For brother Toby, I couldn't have done this without you – M.O.

I dedicate this book to my mum, Rebecca. She never stops believing in me and always reminds me why I'm special. Love you, Mum – M.A.

*All statistics and figures correct at
the time of writing (March 2025)*

First published 2025 by Walker Books Ltd
87 Vauxhall Walk, London SE11 5HJ

2 4 6 8 10 9 7 5 3

Text © 2025 Matt Oldfield and Maggie Alphonsi
Illustrations © 2025 Dan Leydon

The right of Matt Oldfield and Maggie Alphonsi to be identified as authors and of Dan Leydon as illustrator of this work has been asserted in accordance with the Copyright, Designs and Patents Act 1988

EU Authorized Representative: HackettFlynn Ltd
36 Cloch Choirneal, Balrothery, Co. Dublin, K32 C942, Ireland
EU@walkerpublishinggroup.com

This book has been typeset in ITC Leawood

Printed and bound by CPI Group (UK) Ltd, Croydon CR0 4YY

All rights reserved. No part of this book may be reproduced, transmitted or stored in an information retrieval system in any form or by any means, graphic, electronic or mechanical, including photocopying, taping and recording, without prior written permission from the publisher. Additionally, no part of this book may be used or reproduced in any manner for the purpose of training artificial intelligence technologies or systems, nor for text and data mining.

British Library Cataloguing in Publication Data: a catalogue record for this book is available from the British Library

ISBN 978-1-5295-2504-5

www.walker.co.uk

MATT OLDFIELD &
MAGGIE ALPHONSI

illustrated by Dan Leydon

WALKER
BOOKS

CONTENTS

READY FOR RUGBY?	6
1. FRONT ROW	23
Sean Fitzpatrick	30
John Smit	34
Sarah Bern	38
Ox Nché	42
Tadhg Furlong	46
Fiao'o Fa'amausili	50
Front Row Superstars Quiz	54
2. SECOND ROW	57
Alun Wyn Jones	64
Joe McCarthy	68
Manaé Feleu	70
Eben Etzebeth	72
Zoe Aldcroft	76
John Eales	80
Second Row Superstars Quiz	84
3. BACK ROW	87
Richie McCaw	94
Aoife Wafer	98
Pieter-Steph du Toit	102
Grégory Alldritt	106
Alex Matthews	110
Ardie Savea	114
Siya Kolisi	118
Sophie de Goede	122
Back Row Superstars Quiz	126
4. SCRUM-HALF	129
Gareth Edwards	136
George Gregan	140
Cam Roigard	144
Faf de Klerk	148

Antoine Dupont	152
Laure Sansus	156
Agustín Pichot	160
Scrum-Half Superstars Quiz	164
5. FLY-HALF	**167**
Anna Richards	174
Dan Carter	178
Paolo Garbisi	182
Marcus Smith	186
Finn Russell	190
Johnny Sexton	194
Jonny Wilkinson	198
Fly-Half Superstars Quiz	202
6. CENTRES	**205**
Brian O'Driscoll	212
Tana Umaga	216
Tommaso Menoncello	220
Jonathan Danty	222
Emily Scarratt	224
Semi Radradra	228
Gabrielle Vernier	232
Centres Superstars Quiz	236
7. BACK THREE	**239**
Jonah Lomu	246
Bryan Habana	250
Portia Woodman	254
Ellie Kildunne	258
Damian Penaud	262
Duhan van der Merwe	266
Ilona Maher	270
Jason Robinson	274
Shane Williams	278
Back Three Superstars Quiz	282
GAME OVER!	**284**

READY FOR RUGBY?

Hello! We're here to knock you off your feet (in a nice way, don't worry!) with everything you need to know about 50 of rugby's greatest superstars. Rugby is a game that requires many different skills, and so there are lots of different types of superstar in every team. Some are better at tackling, some are better at passing, some are better at running, and some are brilliant at all three. In this book, we've divided our superstars up into seven key positions:

1. **FRONT ROW:** the big, strong scrum soldiers.
2. **SECOND ROW:** the long-armed lineout leaders.
3. **BACK ROW:** the tough, flying flankers and number 8s.
4. **SCRUM-HALF:** the agile pass-masters.
5. **FLY-HALF:** the skilful playmakers.
6. **CENTRES:** the pacy, powerful all-rounders.
7. **BACK THREE:** the lightning-fast wingers and full-backs.

We want to show you a wide range of superstars from all over the world, from both the men's and women's games, so 50 really isn't that many, is it? We could have picked 100, no problem! Each player is unique, but we've also broken them down into categories:

- **LEGEND:** all-time greats
- **RISING STAR:** young megastars
- **MODERN HERO:** champions of today
- **ENTERTAINER:** players with talent and personality
- **GAMECHANGER:** inspirational pioneers.

But before we introduce you to all our incredible superstars, we wanted to start by talking a bit more about the game they play. And who better to talk about it than a true legend of the sport and a Women's Rugby World Cup winner? Meet ...

MAGGIE ALPHONSI!

MAGGIE ALPHONSI

FLANKER

★ LEGEND ★

POSITION **FLANKER (NO. 7)**

DATE OF BIRTH **20 DECEMBER 1983**

COUNTRY **ENGLAND**

CLUBS **SARACENS**

SUPERSTAR MOMENT **WINNING THE 2014 WOMEN'S RUGBY WORLD CUP WITH ENGLAND**

FUN FACT **BEFORE TAKING UP RUGBY AGED FOURTEEN, MAGGIE WAS A TALENTED DISCUS AND SHOT-PUT THROWER AND DREAMED OF REPRESENTING TEAM GB AT THE OLYMPICS.**

MAGGIE ALPHONSI

Maggie is one of the game's greatest superstars! She has 74 caps for England, seven Six Nations titles, one Women's Rugby World Cup win, and a place in the World Rugby Hall of Fame. She was also named the *Sunday Times* Sportswoman of the Year in 2010, and a year later, she became the first female player ever to win the Pat Marshall award for Rugby Union Writers' Personality of the Year!

Maggie played at a time when women's rugby lacked funding and support, and is a pioneer who helped to grow the game. And despite experiencing painful defeats to New Zealand in the Women's Rugby World Cup finals in 2006 and 2010, she kept going until England lifted the trophy at last in 2014. Then, after retiring from the game, Maggie became the first former female player to commentate on men's international rugby on TV.

As a flanker (more on the rugby positions in a minute!), she was most famous for her speed and ferocious tackling, which once floored England men's star Owen Farrell in training and earned her one of the best nicknames in the game: "Maggie the Machine".

✦ WHY I LOVE RUGBY ✦

MAGGIE'S INSIGHTS

I can't wait to share with you my insights into our superstars! I've been so lucky to have a career as a rugby player and a pundit. But first of all, I want to tell you just how much I love playing rugby — the smell of the pitch after the grass has been freshly cut, the feel of the bumpy surface of the rugby ball in my hands, and the roar of the crowd when you run onto the field. Here are my top three reasons why I think it is the greatest game on Earth:

1. It's fun

Rugby always puts a smile on my face. You play alongside your best friends and make new friends. You travel locally, nationally, or if you're really lucky, internationally. I enjoyed the contact of the game, especially when I had the ball and ran into people, causing them to land on their bottoms! (I didn't find it fun when it happened to me, though.) Scoring tries was also very enjoyable. I loved the emotions I got when I grounded the ball over the white try line. It felt amazzzzzziiiiiinnnngggg!

2. You get to play to your strengths

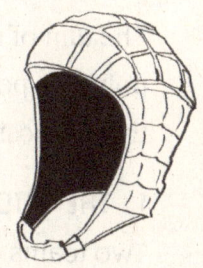

I was always quite big and strong, and I loved to run. I tried lots of different sports — netball, football, rounders, athletics — and I was quite good at all of them, but I didn't fully enjoy any of them. When I found rugby union at the age of fourteen, thanks to my school PE teacher, everything just clicked because there is a place for everyone in the sport, no matter what your shape or size. My strength meant that I could tackle and break through contact. My pace and power meant that I could evade tackles and score tries. When I was growing up, the boys would always think girls could not be strong, or be as good at rugby as them. But I was a tackling machine! When I made a big tackle, it felt like I immediately won the respect of the boys and we were equals. I had finally found a sport that allowed me to be me.

3. It's actually a pretty easy game to play!

Yes, the sport has a lot of rules, but when you get to grips with them, you'll see that the sport is not only a huge amount of fun, but actually really quite simple.

Don't believe me? I'll prove it...

HOW TO PLAY RUGBY IN SIX SUPER-SIMPLE STEPS

The aim of rugby is simple: a team scores as many points as possible, while simultaneously stopping their opposing team scoring.

1. THE PITCH

Two teams of fifteen players meet on a pitch, usually outside on grass. Each team has eight substitute players that sit on the bench. The two teams take up their positions at either end of the pitch.

2. THE START

The game begins when a player from one team drop kicks the ball into the air and towards the opposite end of the field. The game lasts for 80 minutes and the clock is stopped for injuries or substitutions, so no extra time is added at the end, like it is in football.

3. ATTACK

Whoever catches the ball has three options to try and get the ball to the try line at the other end of the pitch:

- to pass it with their hands (YOU ALWAYS HAVE TO PASS BACKWARDS!) to a teammate,
- to kick it with their feet,
- or to run with it in their hands.

4. DEFENCE

The job of the other team is to stop that player with the ball by tackling them off their feet and down on to the ground. And if they can steal (or grab) the ball legally at the same time? Then it's their turn to attack! The referee can award red and yellow cards for foul play.

5. HOW TO SCORE

Both teams are trying to get the ball past their opponents and place it down over the try line at the opponent's end of the pitch – the line with the goalposts. The most common way is for an individual player to break through the defence and touch the ball down to score a **TRY**, which is worth five points. The scoring team then gets the chance to kick the ball over the crossbar and through the goalposts. This is called a **CONVERSION**, and is worth an extra two points.

The other ways to score are by kicking a **PENALTY** or **DROP GOAL** (both are worth three points). A penalty comes when the other team commits a foul. The ball has to be kicked between the posts from the position where the foul was committed.

6. WINNERS

Whichever team finishes with the most points wins the match!

POSITIONS ON THE PITCH

We can divide the fifteen players in a rugby team up into two main groups:

THE FORWARDS

Numbers 1–8: in general, they tend to be bigger and stronger (and they'd probably argue braver, too!).

Main task: defending – tackling (always BELOW THE CHEST, and preferably BELOW THE WAIST too!) and winning the ball back.

You'll find them: further forwards (duh!) on the pitch, pushing in the scrum and jumping, lifting or throwing in the lineout.

Positions: props, hooker, second rowers (or locks), flankers, number 8

THE BACKS

Numbers 9–15: in general, they tend to be smaller in stature and faster (and they'd probably argue more skilful, too!).

Main task: attacking – carrying the ball forwards and scoring tries.

You'll find them: further back (duh!) behind the forwards, but then once they get the ball – ZOOM! – they're off!

Positions: scrum-half, fly-half, centres, wingers, full-back

BUT WHICH KIND OF RUGBY ARE WE TALKING ABOUT?

In this book we're talking about rugby union, but there are also two other major sports with "rugby" in the title: rugby league and rugby sevens. *What?!* we hear you ask. Yes, each sport has its own rules and style of play.

★ RUGBY UNION ★

Rugby union started in Rugby, England, in the early 1800s, with the first international match played between England and Scotland in 1871.

Number of players per team: 15 (with 8 on the bench)

Number of players on each side of the scrum: 8 (in a 3-4-1 formation)

A game lasts: 80 minutes

Scoring: Try (5 points or 7 if conversion kick is successful), penalty or drop goal (3 points)

When a player is tackled, they must: Release the ball, hopefully to a teammate, but players from the other team can try to grab it (as long as they're onside, holding their own body weight and their feet are on the ground)

Style: Physical and tactical

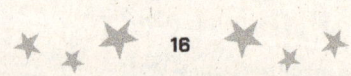

★ RUGBY SEVENS ★

Rugby sevens started in Scotland in the 1880s.
Number of players per team: 7 (with 3 on the bench)
Number of players on each side of the scrum: Only 3, and just in the front row
A game lasts: 14 minutes (7 minutes each half)
Scoring: Try (5 points or 7 if conversion kick is successful), penalty or drop goal (3 points)
When a player is tackled, they must: Do the same as in rugby union
Style: High tempo, lots of running and tries
Rugby sevens superstars who have made a successful switch to rugby union: Jonah Lomu, Ardie Savea, Portia Woodman, Ilona Maher, Virimi Vakatawa, Stacey Waaka
An Olympic sport since: 2016 (both men's and women's)

★ RUGBY LEAGUE ★

Rugby league started in England in 1895.
Number of players per team: 13
Number of players on each side of the scrum: 6 (in a 3-2-1 formation)
A game lasts: 80 minutes
Scoring: Try (4 points or 6 if conversion kick is successful), penalty (2 points), drop goal (1 point)
When a player is tackled, they must: Get up facing forwards and roll the ball back between their legs with their boot. The defence must run back 5 metres before they can move forwards and make a tackle.
Style: Fast and flowing
Rugby league superstars who have made a successful switch to rugby union: Jason Robinson, Semi Radradra, Tana Umaga, Sonny Bill Williams, Lote Tuqiri

TEAMS AND TOURNAMENTS

As with almost all professional team sports, in rugby, superstars play for two different teams at the same time: their club and their country.

However, unlike football, rugby is a sport where the international game is still more popular than the club competitions, and so in this book you'll be hearing a lot about the national teams and their interesting nicknames, such as:

- The Red Roses — England Women's
- The All Blacks — New Zealand Men's
- The Black Ferns — New Zealand Women's
- The Wallabies — Australia Men's
- The Wallaroos — Australia Women's
- The Springboks — South Africa Men's & Women's
- The Pumas — Argentina Men's

International teams compete against each other in one-off games called "Test matches" (or if there are a few of them, "Test series"), and also in different tournaments.

THE SIX NATIONS

The Men's Six Nations is held between January and March every year. The Women's Six Nations is held between March and April and, surprise, surprise, for both competitions there are six national teams involved: England, Scotland, Wales, Ireland, France, and Italy (whose addition made the men's Five Nations the Six Nations in 2000). The men's competition has been running since 1883 (when it was just the four home nations), while the women's event was founded in 1996 (Spain used to compete in it before Italy joined in 2007). From now on, to keep things simple, we'll just call it the Six Nations.

All the teams play each other once (either home or away), and at the end, the team that wins the most games is the winner. If a team wins all five of their matches, it is known as winning a "Grand Slam".

STATS

- The countries with the most Men's Six Nations titles are England and Wales, tied on 39!
- The country with the most Women's Six Nations titles is England with 20.

THE RUGBY CHAMPIONSHIP

The Rugby Championship is held every year, with four teams competing for the trophy: Australia, New Zealand, South Africa and Argentina. The tournament began in 1996, and before Argentina joined in 2012, it was called the Tri Nations Series. Each team plays each other twice (home and away), but if it's a World Cup year, then they only play each other once.

STATS

- The country with the most Rugby Championship (and Tri Nations) titles is New Zealand with 20.

There is no Women's Rugby Championship (yet!), but there is a similar tournament called the Pacific Four Series, played between New Zealand, Australia, USA and Canada. And there's also...

WXV

WXV is a new women's competition held every year, with three different levels: WXV1 for the world's top-ranked teams, WXV2 and WXV3. Each level consists of six teams, and each team plays three matches.

The competition kicked off in 2023, with England winning WXV1, Scotland winning WXV2, and Ireland winning WXV3.

THE RUGBY WORLD CUP

Held every four years since 1987 in the men's game, and 1991 in the women's, the Rugby World Cup is the sport's most famous competition, and it gets bigger every time. There will be 16 national teams at the Women's Rugby World Cup in 2025, and at the next men's tournament in 2027, there will be 24.

After a group stage, the top teams then go through to a knock-out stage, ending with quarter-finals, semi-finals, and then a final.

STATS
- The country which has won the most Men's Rugby World Cup trophies is South Africa with 4.
- The country which has won the most Women's Rugby World Cup trophies is New Zealand with 6.

So far, the schedule should sound like most other major international sports, but there is one extra-special event that's unique to rugby...

THE BRITISH AND IRISH LIONS

Since 1888, a squad of the best men's players from England, Scotland, Wales and Ireland has set off on a tour to either Australia, New Zealand or South Africa to face that country's national team in what is now a three-match series. It's a really big deal in rugby, especially in Britain and Ireland, where it's almost as big as the World Cup itself.

What's even more exciting is that, finally, a British and Irish Lions women's team has been launched and will tour New Zealand in 2027. It's super cool and will make history!

SAY HELLO TO YOUR SUPERSTARS

So, are you ready to say hello to our 50 rugby heroes? Each of their stories is filled with interesting stats, funny facts, inspiring moments, and, of course, exciting sporting drama! And at the end of each section, there's a quiz, so you can find out exactly what kind of rugby superstar you would be.

Even better, Maggie is going to share all her expert knowledge about each player and their position. Look out for her insights at the end of each profile to learn from a World-Cup winner!

Got it so far? Good, now it's time to welcome our first group of players onto the pitch ... our fantastic front row.

1. FRONT ROW
THE FORWARDS

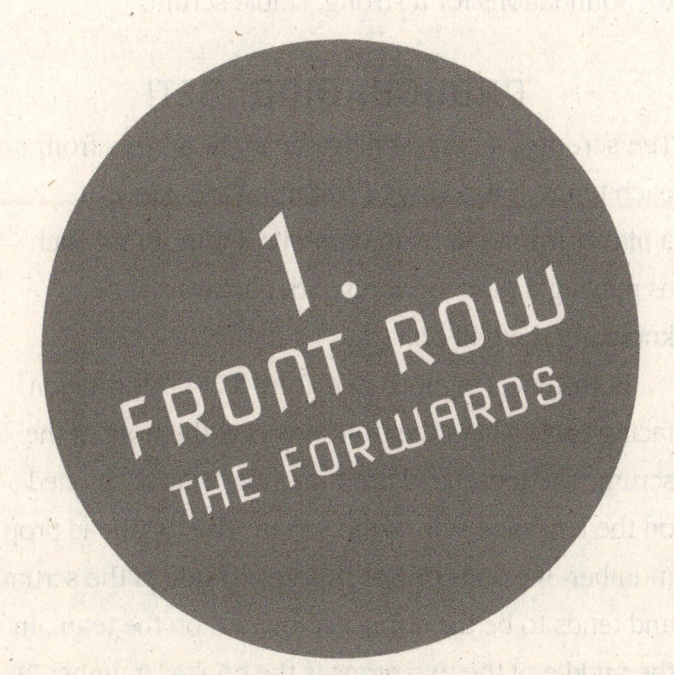

Right, let's kick things off with numbers 1, 2 and 3: the loosehead prop, the hooker and the tighthead prop. These three positions form the front row and the foundations for a strong, stable scrum.

CROUCH, BIND, SET!

The scrum is a contest between eight players from each team. It is a way of restarting the game, if a player from one team commits a minor foul such as playing a pass forwards (not backwards) or knocking the ball on.

Both sets of eight players form a 3-4-1 formation, facing each other. The front row is at the front of the scrum. The loosehead prop (number 1) is positioned on the left-hand side of the scrum. The tighthead prop (number 3) stands on the right-hand side of the scrum and tends to be the strongest forward on the team. In the middle of the two props is the hooker (number 2).

When the scrum is called, the hooker stands in the middle, puts an arm around the prop on either side, and the front row bind together, holding on to each other somewhere between armpit and hip. They then wait for the referee's instructions:

- **"Crouch!"** Everyone gets into their low positions, ready to go, with the front row

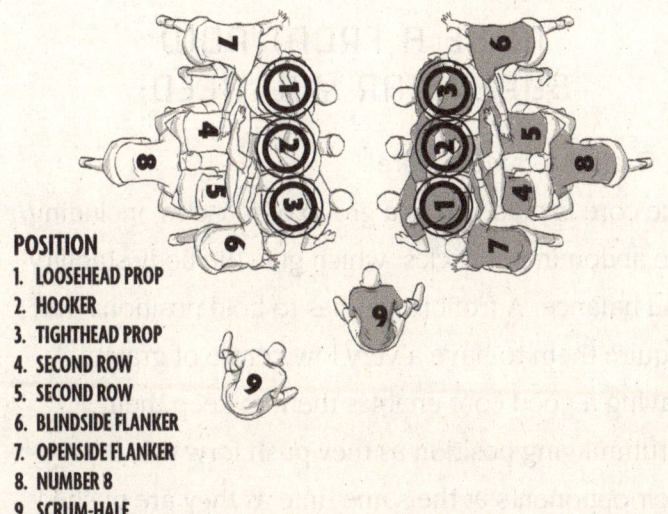

POSITION
1. LOOSEHEAD PROP
2. HOOKER
3. TIGHTHEAD PROP
4. SECOND ROW
5. SECOND ROW
6. BLINDSIDE FLANKER
7. OPENSIDE FLANKER
8. NUMBER 8
9. SCRUM-HALF

bending forwards at the waist, and the second and back rows crouching down behind them.

🏉 **"Bind!"** The two sets of players move towards each other and form a tight pack of 16.

🏉 **"Set!"** It's time for the two sets of players to push forwards against each other.

The ball is then put into the middle of the scrum by the scrum-half of the team who won the foul. Each team competes for the ball. The hooker has to keep possession by "hooking" the ball back with one foot, so it can exit the scrum for the waiting scrum-half (or back row player, normally the number 8) to launch an attack.

TO BE A FRONT ROW SUPERSTAR YOU NEED:

1. A strong, stable core

The core is made up of a group of muscles, including the abdominal muscles, which give the body stability and balance. A front rower has to hold positions that require them to have a very low centre of gravity. Having a good core enables them to keep their scrummaging position as they push forwards into their opponents at the same time as they are pushed from behind by their teammates.

2. All-round strength

A front rower needs to have massive leg strength to help them push in the scrum, plus a powerful back and neck so they can stay low and rigid. They also need to have strong shoulders, arms and glutes (bottom) muscles for lifting players and holding them up in the air at **lineouts**.

3. Bravery

A front rower must be fearless and willing to go head first to connect with the opposite front row in the scrum. Once they engage, they have to push with all their might and believe that they can physically outdo their opponent.

RUGBY RULES

A <u>LINEOUT</u> happens when the ball goes into touch (out of play). It is a set-piece contest between anywhere from two to thirteen players on each team, but most commonly four and seven. The aim is simple: to catch the ball, or pass off the top of the jump to a receiver, and get your team on the attack. The two groups of players form two lines next to each other five metres out from the touchline, and wait for the referee's whistle.

The hooker (it almost always is this position, but it doesn't have to be) throws the ball down the middle of the lineout, into the space between the two lined-up teams. The forwards for each team lift their jumper (often a second rower) into the air to try and win the ball. The hooker needs a powerful and accurate throw so the jumper can catch the ball, and the players in the lineout need to be really strong to lift the jumper into the air.

STAYING POWER

Because they're so big and strong (and maybe also because they don't do quite as much running as the backs), front rowers often stay fit and play a lot of matches.

STATS

- Hooker **Agustín Creevy** (2005–23) is Argentina's most-capped player and sits joint-second on the list of most appearances at a Men's Rugby World Cup.
- Hooker **Fiao'o Fa'amausili** (2002–18) is second on the all-time appearance list for the New Zealand women's team.

LEADING FROM THE FRONT

The front rowers are powerful, reliable and at the forefront of everything. For those reasons, they often make excellent captains, especially hookers:

1997–2006
Farah Palmer captained New Zealand, they won three Women's Rugby World Cups and lost only one match.

2007
John Smit led South Africa to Men's Rugby World Cup glory.

2016
Dylan Hartley led England to a Men's Six Nations Grand Slam, their first since 2003.

THE FRONT ROW THEN ...

The front row used to be a place for the heaviest players, who – no offence! – weren't always the fittest members of the team. They pushed in the scrum and made a few tackles, but if someone passed them the ball when their team was attacking? Ah, pass it straight on again!

... V. THE FRONT ROW NOW

In the modern game, front rowers are often much fitter and faster (although they're still often substituted after 50 minutes). They still need to be excellent in the scrum and lineout, but they're also expected to get the ball and carry it forwards towards the try line.

SO, WHICH KIND OF FRONT ROWER WOULD YOU BE?

Will you be more power and push, or speed and skill? Are you an unstoppable scrum champion, or a try-scoring machine? Or maybe you'll be the front row superstar who can do it all!

To help you decide, here's a look at six of the greatest front rowers rugby has ever seen, all with different styles and approaches. Then take our quiz to find out which superstar you would be.

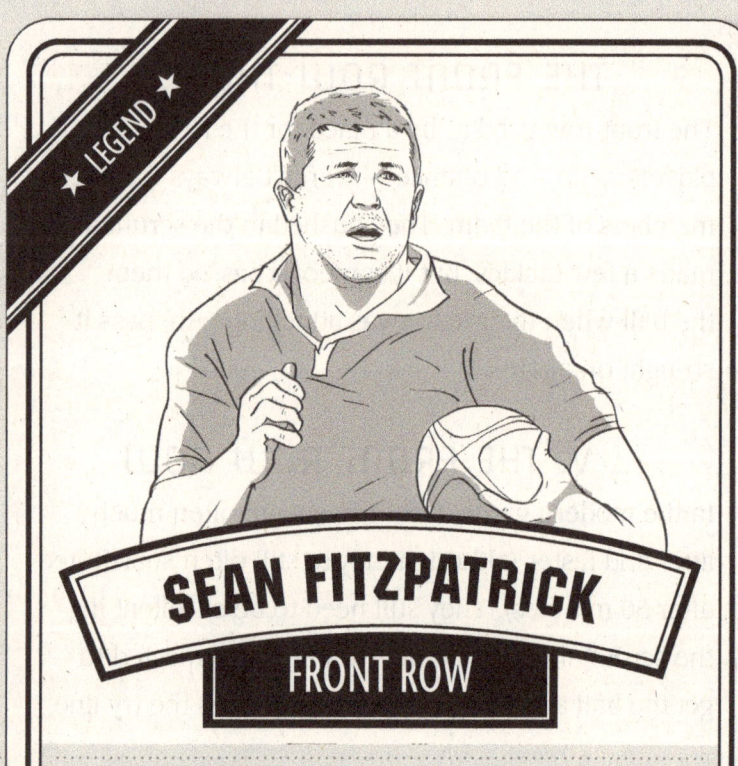

SEAN FITZPATRICK

FRONT ROW

POSITION **HOOKER**

DATE OF BIRTH **4 JUNE 1963**

COUNTRY **NEW ZEALAND**

CLUBS **AUCKLAND, AUCKLAND BLUES**

SUPERSTAR MOMENT **WINNING THE FIRST-EVER MEN'S RUGBY WORLD CUP IN 1987**

FUN FACT **ACROSS HIS 92 TEST APPEARANCES, SEAN WAS ONLY A SUBSTITUTE ONCE: IN HIS VERY LAST MATCH!**

SEAN FITZPATRICK

Sean Fitzpatrick was born to play rugby – his dad, Brian, was a famous international player. Brian had been a speedy back, but Sean decided he was better suited to the front row. And with his power and perseverance, it turned out to be the perfect fit.

After starting out in club rugby in Auckland, Sean got his first international call-up in 1986, when a young New Zealand side, nicknamed "The Baby Blacks", played a Test series in France. He played well and his team won, but Sean didn't become his country's first-choice hooker straight away. New Zealand's captain, Andy Dalton, played that position, so Sean was a substitute.

Oh well, it gave him time to learn. He built all his skills, but worked particularly hard at becoming more and more accurate at throwing the ball hard and straight in each and every lineout.

Just before the first-ever Men's Rugby World Cup in 1987, Sean's opportunity came. Dalton suffered a training injury, which meant Sean suddenly moved into the New Zealand All Blacks starting line-up. Hurray! With the pressure on, he played brilliantly. The All Blacks stormed through to the final. By then, Dalton was back to full fitness, but the coach, Brian Lochore, stuck with Sean, who played his part as New Zealand beat France 29–9. They were the first official Men's Rugby World Cup champions!

It was an unforgettable day for Sean, and there would be plenty more to come as the All Blacks went on a record-breaking run of 23 Test matches without defeat. No, he wasn't an exciting, try-scoring superstar, but Sean was exactly what you want from a great front rower: solid and reliable. He even set a new rugby world record of his own by playing 63 Test matches in a row!

In 1992, Sean received one of rugby's greatest honours: he was named as the new All Blacks captain! And it was a role he held until his last international match against Wales in 1997.

It wasn't all just success after success for Sean, though. He had to bounce back from some major disappointments along the way. Perhaps the biggest was the Men's Rugby World Cup in 1995. New Zealand were the favourites to lift the Webb Ellis Cup (the trophy awarded to the winner of the tournament) again, but this time they were beaten in the final by the hosts South Africa, 15–12 in extra-time. For Sean, his dream of lifting the trophy as captain had been cruelly crushed, but he didn't give up. A year later, he had his revenge when he led New Zealand to a stunning series win in South Africa for the first time ever.

When Sean wrote a book about his life in 2011, he called it *Winning Matters: Being the Best You Can Be*. Eight words that really sum him up as an ultimate rugby superstar.

MAGGIE'S INSIGHTS

I remember watching an interview with Sean, where he talked about what it was like to lose to South Africa in the final. He called it "the one that got away". The interview struck a chord with me because it reminded me of the many finals my England team had been runners-up in — there will always be ones that get away! I also had the privilege to work with Sean in 2015, as a pundit on the Men's Rugby World Cup when I made my broadcasting debut. He was so natural and it immediately put me at ease, and we have remained friends and colleagues ever since.

★ LEGEND ★

JOHN SMIT
FRONT ROW

POSITION **HOOKER, PROP (TIGHTHEAD)**

DATE OF BIRTH **3 APRIL 1978**

COUNTRY **SOUTH AFRICA**

CLUBS **SHARKS, CLERMONT, SARACENS**

SUPERSTAR MOMENT **CAPTAINING HIS COUNTRY TO WORLD CUP GLORY IN 2007**

FUN FACT **JOHN IS ALSO A BIG TENNIS FAN. "A BUCKET-LIST ITEM OF MINE WAS TO PLAY AT WIMBLEDON BUT RUGBY RUINED THAT DREAM!" HE ONCE SAID.**

JOHN SMIT

Right, let's go straight from one front row leader to another. Just as Sean Fitzpatrick was retiring from international rugby in 1997, a young South African front rower was playing his first games for the University of Natal. His name? John Smit, or "Barney" as he would be known throughout his professional career, for no good reason.

John actually started out as a tighthead prop, playing for the South Africa youth teams. In 1999, however, he moved into the middle of the front row to play hooker instead. He had the right skills for the role – real power in the scrum, and an accurate throw for lineouts.

With older players retiring, South Africa also needed hookers. And John was up for it: "Pick me, I'll do it!" he said. A year later, he made his senior debut for South Africa's Springboks. For the first few years, however, John mostly came off the bench, playing back-up to Danie Coetzee. That all changed in 2004, however, when Jake White became the South Africa coach. He was looking for a new captain for his team, and he believed that John was the right man for the job. Not only was he a great player, but he was also a great organizer and he already led by example, both on and off the rugby pitch. Perfect!

And White was right, John made a great captain. Between 2003 and 2007, he played 46 Test matches in a row, setting a new South African record. His run came to an end in June 2007, when he injured his hamstring just months before the 2007 Men's Rugby World Cup in France. In typical style, John came storming back just in time to lead his team at the tournament.

Scoring his first-ever World Cup try in the quarter-finals against Fiji was a proud moment for John, but his greatest achievement was bringing all of the South Africa players together, creating a family feel within the squad. That team spirit was crucial as they battled past Argentina in the semi-finals, and then England in the final. When the last whistle blew, John threw his arms in the air and then wrapped them around his teammates. Together, they had done it: South Africa had won the ultimate prize – a Rugby World Cup!

As well as the trophy and his winner's medal, John also ended the tournament with a record that all hookers dream of: a 100 per cent accuracy rating for his lineout throws!

Reliable, hard-working, powerful, inspirational – as both a front rower and a leader, John was all of those things and more. He was also talented and humble enough to switch positions again, midway through his international career. In 2008, when South Africa wanted to give another hooker, Bismarck du Plessis, a go, John agreed to move to play tighthead prop for thirteen Test matches. Now that's a real team player!

John retired from international rugby after the 2011 Men's Rugby World Cup, as South Africa's most-capped men's player and their longest-standing captain.

John took South Africa to a second World Cup title in 2007, when the pressure was on the nation to back up what they had famously done in 1995. After that long wait, through his leadership they were able to finally get it over the line. He was also unique because he could play prop, too. That's not something you see much these days because it is such a tough skill to master.

★ RISING STAR ★

SARAH BERN
FRONT ROW

POSITION **PROP (TIGHTHEAD)**

DATE OF BIRTH **10 JULY 1997**

COUNTRY **ENGLAND**

CLUBS **GLOUCESTER-HARTPURY, BRISTOL BEARS**

SUPERSTAR MOMENT **SCORING A CRUCIAL TRY IN THE 2017 WOMEN'S RUGBY WORLD CUP SEMI-FINALS**

FUN FACT **SARAH'S DAD, GRAEME, PLAYED VOLLEYBALL FOR SCOTLAND!**

SARAH BERN

Sport-loving Sarah grew up in south-west London. When she was eleven years old, her cousin started training with local club London Irish, and so she joined too, and became the only girl in a boys' team.

At first, some boys refused to pass the ball to her, but Sarah was determined to prove herself – and she succeeded! During warm-up one day, a coach told her to tackle him as hard as she could. When she did, the coach went flying! "Oh, you're quite good, aren't you?" he acknowledged.

After that, Sarah moved on to play for the girls' teams at Esher Rugby Club, where she starred as a speedy, try-scoring centre (number 12 or 13) before switching to become a powerful back row forward (number 6, 7 or 8). Playing in her new position, Sarah became so unstoppable that in 2015, she was called up for the England Under-20s.

A year later, the England senior team was looking for more front rowers, in particular a new tighthead prop. Would Sarah be up for switching positions again?

At first, Sarah said no, but as the 2017 Women's Rugby World Cup got close, she thought, *Why not?* If this was her best chance to play for her country at the highest level, then she had to take it. She set about working hard to learn all the key skills needed for a tighthead prop.

At the tournament in Ireland, Sarah shone as the youngest member of the England squad. She gave a player-of the-match performance in the semi-finals against France, where she dominated in the scrum, tackled brilliantly, and even powered her way over the line to score a crucial try. What a superstar!

Sadly, England went on to lose to New Zealand in the final, but for Sarah it was a great beginning. In 2019, she was named England Women's Player of the Year and shortlisted for World Rugby Women's Player of the Year after helping the Red Roses win a Grand Slam at the Women's Six Nations. Along the way, she scored five tries, including an incredible run against Wales. "That is just ridiculous," the TV commentator cheered. "Tightheads are not supposed to score tries like that!"

Despite her front row position, Sarah was determined not to change her natural game. "I love attacking and if I can get the opportunity to get my hands on the ball," she said in 2023, "it's probably the thing I love most about rugby."

Those words came after perhaps Sarah's greatest attacking performance, in England's 68–5 victory over Italy. If it wasn't for the number 3 on the back of her shirt, you would have thought she was still a centre, or even a winger, as she raced forwards again and again, skipping past tackles and setting up two tries for her teammates.

Sarah is currently the world's best tighthead prop in the women's game. I had the privilege of coaching her in her early years and even back then she was a standout. She was always so confident. I remember her challenging me to an arm wrestle — and she beat me! I still haven't lived it down. She was always very strong and always committed to getting better and improving her craft. She's come so far in her career and I'm excited to see where she can go.

★ MODERN HERO ★

OX NCHÉ
FRONT ROW

POSITION **PROP (LOOSEHEAD)**

DATE OF BIRTH **23 JULY 1995**

COUNTRY **SOUTH AFRICA**

CLUBS **FREE STATE CHEETAHS, SHARKS**

SUPERSTAR MOMENT **WINNING THE 2023 MEN'S RUGBY WORLD CUP**

FUN FACT **OX HAS A SISTER WHO IS ALSO A RUGBY PLAYER, AND GUESS WHAT SHE CALLS HERSELF! FOX!**

OX NCHÉ

A super-powerful rugby player called "Ox", who does lots of pushing on the pitch? Really?! Sadly, it's not his real first name, that is Retshegofaditswe. But "Ox" is pretty awesome, isn't it? It's also a nickname he shares with a legendary South African loosehead prop from the past: Os du Randt.

So, would the new Ox go on to follow in the sturdy studmarks of the old Ox? After starting for South Africa at the 2015 World Rugby Under-20 Championship, Retshegofaditswe collected his first senior international cap in June 2018. But after losing on his debut against Wales, he didn't play for his country again for the next three years.

Ox was disappointed, of course, but he didn't give up. He kept working hard on his game, and in 2020, he switched clubs, moving from his home team, the Free State Cheetahs, to the Sharks (they love their animal names in South Africa!). That turned out to be a brilliant decision because playing for a new team in a new part of the country, he came into his own. In 2021, Ox was finally called up for South Africa again, and since then, he hasn't looked back.

In terms of his size, Ox is the classic old-school front rower: quite small in height (172.5 cm), but mighty in weight (114 kg). In terms of his personality, however, he is very much a modern hero. He's famous for his funny Instagram posts and in particular his catchphrase:

"SALADS DON'T WIN SCRUMS!"

You can even buy T-shirts with those words written across them! In another catchphrase, he puts his success down to chocolate caramel cake:

"I DON'T COUNT CALORIES, I COUNT SLICES!"

But let's get back to his strengths on the pitch. That winning mix of a low centre of gravity and incredible strength has helped make him one of the best scrummagers in world rugby. Sometimes, he starts for South Africa, but often he's used as a super-sub, part of their powerful replacement front row that's known as "The Bomb Squad".

With his opponents tiring, it's Ox's job to turn the game by dominating the scrum. He did this most brilliantly during South Africa's 2023 Men's Rugby World Cup semi-final against England. He came on to replace Steven Kitshoff in the 49th minute, when his team was losing 12–6, and it quickly became 15–6 after an Owen Farrell England drop goal. Oh dear, were the Springboks heading for a surprise defeat?

No, with Ox pushing them forwards with all his power, South Africa came fighting back. After a successful scrum and then lineout, RG Snyman scored a try to make it 15–13, and then in the final moments of the match, Ox won his biggest battle of all. With one last scrum masterclass, he earned his team a penalty, which Handré Pollard kicked for victory: with the final score as 15–16 to South Africa.

South Africa went on to beat New Zealand in the final, and lift the trophy for the fourth time. Ox was officially a World Champion! Now that deserves a massive chocolate caramel cake!

MAGGIE'S INSIGHTS

Ox is known for being a formidable scrummager. He may not always play a full match, but by coming off the bench he brings a load of energy, which has an amazingly positive impact in the scrum. He is a World Cup winner who continues to make a name for himself.

★ ENTERTAINER ★

TADHG FURLONG
FRONT ROW

POSITION **PROP (TIGHTHEAD)**

DATE OF BIRTH **14 NOVEMBER 1992**

COUNTRY **IRELAND**

CLUB **LEINSTER**

SUPERSTAR MOMENT **WINNING THE SIX NATIONS GRAND SLAM IN 2018 AND 2023**

FUN FACT **AS A YOUNG PLAYER, TADHG GAVE HIMSELF A NEW NICKNAME: "THE JUKEBOX". WHY? "BECAUSE THE HITS KEEP COMING!"**

TADHG FURLONG

Meet Tadhg Furlong, the modern front rower who really can do it all:

- 🏉 push powerfully in the scrum,
- 🏉 stop opponents with stunning tackles,
- 🏉 lift huge teammates high in the lineouts,
- 🏉 AND carry the ball forwards with speed and skill.

The secret to Tadhg's success? Spuds! The Leinster nutritionist Daniel Davey explains: "Tadhg loves his potatoes. He might be having six or ten potatoes a day. So then, I have to say, 'Tadhg, you're having too many potatoes.'"

Really? No, there has to be more to it – let's delve a bit deeper... Tadhg grew up in Wexford, in the South-East of Ireland, working on the family dairy farm, which he now runs himself. A skinny child, he built himself up with sausages and black pudding, and playing PlayStation games! Tadhg and his older brother Eoin used to sit around playing for hours and hours. In the end, their parents had to take the PlayStation away because, in Tadhg's own words, "we were getting big as bulls"!

So that explains his size and strength, but what about Tadhg's speed and skill? There are three reasons for that:

1. He had an excellent rugby education at the Leinster Academy in Dublin.
2. He grew up watching his childhood hero, Keith Wood, a hooker who loved to run with the ball.
3. He spent years playing Irish sports Gaelic football and hurling.

The result is that as well as being big and strong, Tadhg also has the slick hands to play brilliant, swift passes. He even did this in the snow during the 2018 Men's Six Nations match against England. Plus, he has the nimble feet to sidestep multiple opponents, as he did against Scotland in 2021. While Tadhg doesn't score that many tries himself, he loves to be creative and get involved in the build-up play. He's also a very useful kicker, sometimes even practising kicks before matches!

But Tadhg's skills aren't just for show; he uses them to help his team win. Ever since he made his senior international debut just before the 2015 Men's Rugby World Cup, he's been a key part of the

Ireland side and all of their greatest successes: two Men's Six Nations Grand Slams in 2018 and 2023, and the five famous victories over the mighty New Zealand All Blacks between 2016 and 2022.

Tadhg has also been a very important player for the British and Irish Lions, starting every Test match on the tours in 2017 (New Zealand) and 2021 (South Africa). And for his club team, Leinster, he has won the United Rugby Championship (or what was the Pro 12/14) four times, as well as the European Rugby Champions Cup in 2018.

Strength and skill, defence and attack, meat and potatoes – what an incredible combo! Tadhg really is no ordinary front rower.

Tadhg is arguably the best male tighthead prop in the world. Light on his toes and solid in the scrum, he changed the way props are now seen because he has it all. He is comfortable with the ball in hand and is unfazed by being in open play. I love watching him play. It's like watching a back in a forward's jersey!

— MAGGIE'S INSIGHTS

GAMECHANGER

FIAO'O FA'AMAUSILI

FRONT ROW

POSITION **HOOKER**

DATE OF BIRTH **30 SEPTEMBER 1980**

COUNTRY **NEW ZEALAND**

CLUB **AUCKLAND STORM**

SUPERSTAR MOMENT **WINNING THE WOMEN'S RUGBY WORLD CUP FOUR TIMES!**

FUN FACT **AFTER RETIRING FROM RUGBY, FIAO'O IS NOW DOING HER SECOND DREAM JOB: POLICE DETECTIVE!**

FIAO'O FA'AMAUSILI

We'll finish this front row section with one of rugby's most inspiring superstars. Fiao'o was born in Samoa, a small country in the central South Pacific Ocean, but at the age of five, she moved to Auckland, New Zealand, with her family. Through determination and talent, Fiao'o went on to make history for her new country.

But amazingly, Fiao'o was only introduced to rugby, New Zealand's national sport, when she was fifteen years old. She played for the first time during a PE session at her school and was hooked. "I just loved the contact," she said years later. "I've always been quite physical. Like in netball, I was fairly rough. I loved that game, but there was something special about rugby."

After leaving school, aged seventeen, Fiao'o joined the Otahuhu women's team, where she discovered her perfect position: hooker. Then, when she moved to Auckland Marist, she had the chance to play alongside Davida White, who was a Black Fern, a member of New Zealand's women's rugby team. Fiao'o began to dream that, with work, she could become a Black Fern, too!

By 2002, that dream had come true. She was selected in the New Zealand squad for that year's Women's Rugby World Cup, making her international debut in Barcelona against Australia. The Black Ferns won and they made it all the way to the final again, where they beat England 19–9. *Woah*, Fiao'o was a World Cup winner already!

That was only the start, though. For now, Fiao'o was happy to be New Zealand's backup hooker, behind the team captain, Farah Palmer, but she was determined to become her country's first choice. So she worked hard to get stronger in the scrum and in the tackle, to be even better at carrying the ball, and to make her lineout throws even more accurate. Finally, after Palmer announced that she was retiring from international rugby after the 2006 Women's Rugby World Cup, Fiao'o had her chance to shine...

By the time the 2010 Women's Rugby World Cup came around, Fiao'o was not only New Zealand's first-choice hooker, but she was also one of the best players in women's rugby. She kicked off the tournament with back-to-back tries against South Africa and Australia, and then played a key role as the Black Ferns beat France in the semis, and England in the final.

It was another proud moment, and there were even more to come. In 2012, Fiao'o took over as New Zealand captain and after a disappointing performance at the 2014 tournament, her Black Ferns came roaring back to win the Women's Rugby World Cup again in 2017. During the tournament, Fiao'o also celebrated another great personal achievement: she became the first Black Fern to reach 50 caps. She was a national hero and there was still one more final sporting honour to come in 2022, after her retirement: a well-deserved spot in the World Rugby Hall of Fame.

MAGGIE'S INSIGHTS

Fiao'o is an ultimate gamechanger. I remember playing her in the 2006 and 2010 Women's Rugby World Cup finals. She was always a formidable player. She never took a backwards step and it's no surprise that she went on to achieve so much in her rugby career. She has left a legacy and also continues to inspire many women and girls to keep striving for their dreams!

★ QUIZ ★

ARE YOU A LOUD, PROUD LEADER OR DO YOU PREFER TO LET YOUR POWER DO THE TALKING?

LOUD, PROUD LEADER

Would you say you're a one-position player, or are you happy to help out wherever you're needed?

HAPPY TO HELP OUT WHEREVER

You're ... JOHN SMIT! Reliable, hard-working, powerful, inspirational; you'll do anything to help your team to win.

ONE-POSITION PLAYER

LET YOUR POWER DO THE TALKING

Are you all about the scrum or do you love to play ball too?

ALL ABOUT THE SCRUM

You're ... OX NCHÉ! "Salads don't win scrums", but with your super-strength, you definitely do!

LOVE TO PLAY BALL TOO

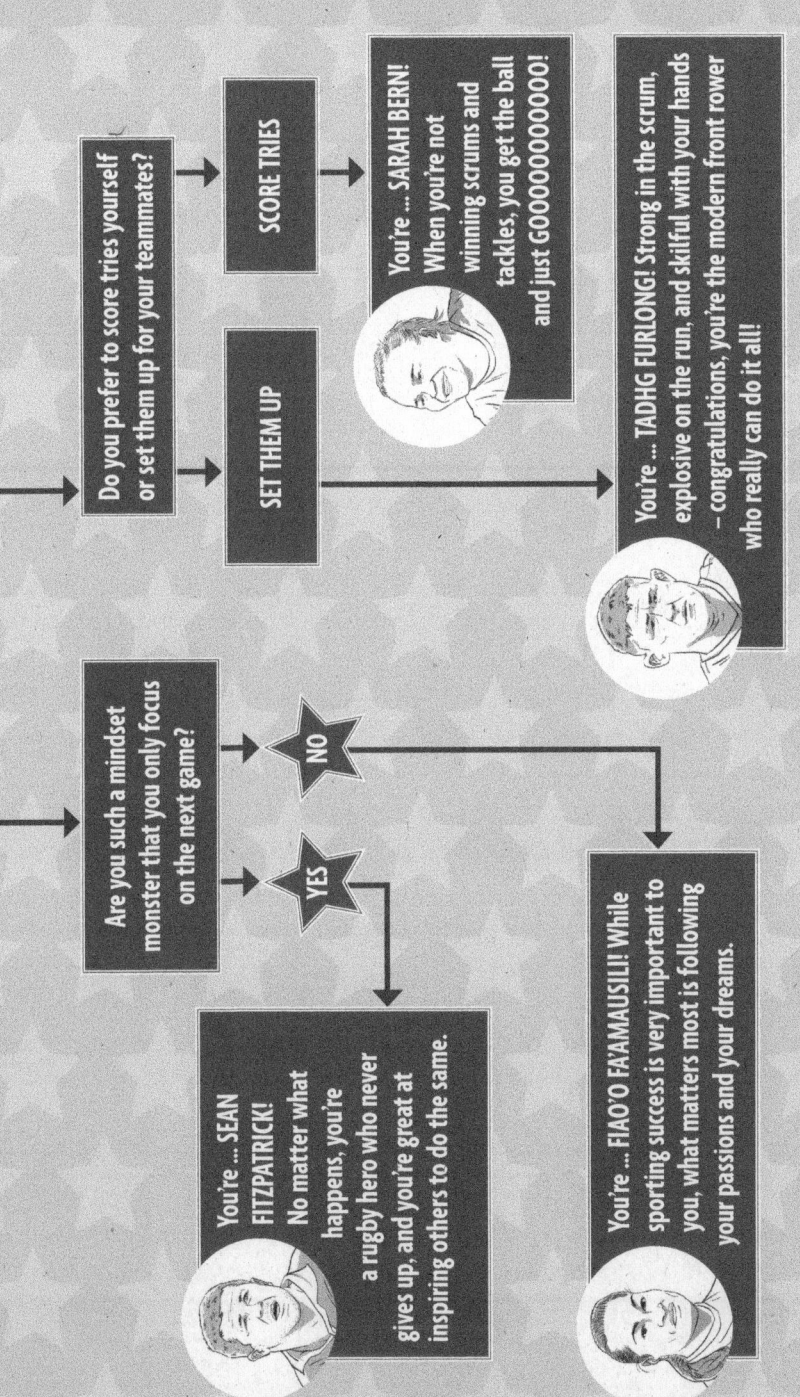

2.
SECOND ROW
THE FORWARDS

Behind the front row of the scrum, you will find two (very tall) players wearing the numbers 4 and 5 shirts. These players form the second row.

THE TEAM ENGINE

The second row is known as the "engine room", because it's their job to push and power their team to victory in lots of different ways:

- **In the lineout:** in modern rugby, a second rower has a very specific role within the team as one of the main lineout jumpers. They have to be lifted high into the air to catch the ball thrown back into play by the hooker.
- **In the scrum:** second rowers are also known as "locks" because when they crouch down and bind to the front row, they lock the scrum into a stable position. Then they drive low and hard to try and win the ball for their team.
- **All over the pitch:** second rowers also have to run around tackling and hitting **rucks** and **mauls**. Rucks and mauls are like less organized scrums; a chance for players from both teams to battle for the ball. Any player in any position can get involved in them, but you'll usually find the second rowers at the centre!

RUGBY RULES

RUCKS AND MAULS

A RUCK starts when a player is tackled and the ball is on the ground, with one or more players from each team, who should be on their feet, competing for it. Players must not handle the ball in the ruck, and must use their feet to move the ball or drive over it so that it emerges at the foot of the player at the back of the ruck, at which point it can be picked up.

A MAUL starts when a player holding the ball is held on their feet, by one or more opponents AND has another player from their own team bound onto them. The team in possession of the ball can then drive their opponents back towards their try line, with the ball passing between players in the maul until eventually someone breaks off and runs away with it.

TO BE A SECOND ROW SUPERSTAR YOU NEED:

1. Long arms and legs (well, a long body, really!)
Being tall is a crucial part of being a second rower. Players use their height to win a ball in a lineout, and if they've got the advantage of being taller than their opponent, they can dominate the lineout and win possession for their team.

2. Rapid reactions
The best second rowers are good at predicting what the opposition are going to do in a lineout. They are quick to react and jump in the air based on what they see the opposition is about to do.

3. Wonderful work-rate
Second rowers may be tall and big in stature, but they never stop moving. These athletes are great at getting around the field, carrying the ball forwards and rushing into every ruck and maul. Second rowers are hard workers and are not afraid of getting stuck in.

STANDING TALL

TOP 3 TALLEST MEN'S INTERNATIONAL RUGBY PLAYERS

RICHARD METCALFE	DEVIN TONER	MARTIN BAYFIELD
Scotland (2000–01)	Ireland (2010–20)	England (1991–96)
2.13 metres (7 ft)	2.10 metres (6 ft 11 in)	2.9 metres (6 ft 10 in)

TOP 3 TALLEST WOMEN'S INTERNATIONAL RUGBY PLAYERS

MARIE LOUISE "MAZ" REILLY	MADOUSSOU FALL	GRACE KEMP
Ireland (2010–present)	Australia (2022–present)	Australia (2022–present)
1.94 metres (6 ft 4 in)	1.87 metres (6 ft 2 in)	1.87 metres (6 ft 2 in)

TOWERS OF TOUGHNESS

As well as being big and strong, second rowers also have a reputation for being fearless and fearsome. Don't try this stuff at home!

- The story goes that legendary New Zealand second row **Sir Colin Meads** (1957–71) used to train by running up mountains with a sheep under each arm!

- France second row **Alain Estève** (1971–75) was so tough he was called the "Beast of Béziers". His idea of a warm-up was to practice headbutts on walls before games!

POWERFUL PARTNERSHIPS

To help their team to win, the two players in the second row have to work together. The best partnerships in rugby history are often formed when one second rower leads on the lineout while the other dominates in the tackle:

LONG-ARMED LINEOUT LEADER **BIG, BASHING POWERHOUSE**

VICTOR MATFIELD **BAKKIES BOTHA**

(2002–14)

Played 63 Tests together for South Africa, winning the 2007 Men's Rugby World Cup

---

LONG-ARMED LINEOUT LEADER **BIG, BASHING POWERHOUSE**

VICTORIA HEIGHWAY **MONALISA CODLING**

(2000–10)

Played together for New Zealand, winning a hat-trick of Women's Rugby World Cups in 2002, 2006, and 2010

LONG-ARMED LINEOUT LEADER **BIG, BASHING POWERHOUSE**

SAM WHITELOCK **BRODIE RETALLICK**

(2012–23)

Played a record 65 Tests together for New Zealand, winning the 2015 Men's Rugby World Cup

To build a successful second row partnership, it also really helps when players know each other really well.

STATS

- **Martin Johnson** and **Ben Kay** played over 200 times together for club (Leicester Tigers) and country (England), including winning the Men's Rugby World Cup in 2003.
- New Zealand pair **Alana** and **Chelsea Bremner** are – yep, you guessed it – sisters!

SO, WHICH KIND OF SECOND ROWER WOULD YOU BE?

Will you be a long-armed lineout leader, or a big, bashing powerhouse? How will you push your team to victory: in the scrum, in the ruck, or on the run? Or maybe you'll be the second-row superstar who can do it all!

To help you decide, here's a look at six of the greatest second rowers rugby has ever seen, all with different styles and approaches. Then take our quiz to find out which superstar you would be.

★ LEGEND ★

ALUN WYN JONES

SECOND ROW

POSITION **SECOND ROW (LOCK)**

DATE OF BIRTH **19 SEPTEMBER 1985**

COUNTRY **WALES**

CLUBS **SWANSEA, OSPREYS, TOULON**

SUPERSTAR MOMENT **CAPTAINING HIS COUNTRY TO A SIX NATIONS GRAND SLAM IN 2019**

FUN FACT **NOT A FUN FACT EXACTLY, BUT AN IMPORTANT ONE: ALUN'S SURNAME IS NOT "WYN JONES"; IT'S JUST "JONES"! WYN IS PART OF HIS FIRST NAME.**

ALUN WYN JONES

The average professional rugby career lasts about seven years, and at international level, it's much shorter. So to play for your country for seventeen years? Unbelievable. Take a bow, AWJ!

As a boy growing up in Mumbles, South Wales, Alun Wyn's first love was football, but that all changed once he started playing rugby at primary school. Later, he trained with the Ospreys Academy, in nearby Swansea, making his debut in their first team in 2005. That year, he also won a Grand Slam with Wales at the Under-21 Six Nations Championship. His next step was breaking into the senior team, but it wasn't going to be easy…

Wales already had lots of fantastic forwards: captain Ryan Jones, flankers Martyn Williams and Colin Charvis, and in the second row, Ian Gough and Robert Sidoli. No problem – for his first senior cap against Argentina, Alun Wyn played as a flanker instead! After that, however, he moved back to his normal position and he soon made the Wales number 5 shirt his own.

From his debut in 2006, to his retirement in 2023, Alun Wyn played a record-breaking 158 Test matches for his country (plus twelve more for the British and Irish Lions), and won the Six Nations five times, including three Grand Slams. He was nominated for World Rugby Men's Player of the Year twice, in 2015 and 2019.

So, how did he shine in top-level rugby for so long? Well, it's a combination of lots of things, of course, but we'll focus on three key ingredients:

1. Hard work

Ask any of Alun Wyn's teammates and they'll all say the same thing: he trained as hard as he played, and he played *really* hard. Throughout his career, he was always looking for ways to improve his game, and to keep himself super-fit, from doing yoga to using oxygen chambers. That relentless drive also rubbed off on those around him, making him an excellent team leader.

2. Consistency

Instead of being spectacular at one thing, Alun Wyn was solidly excellent at every part of the second-row skill set: scrummaging, tackling, rucking, ball-carrying, lineout jumping and lifting. But probably his greatest strength was his consistency: his ability to perform with the same high energy and effort in match after match after match.

3. Toughness

Warning: to reach 170 international caps in a really physical sport like rugby, you have to play through *a lot* of pain. In 2021, Alun Wyn was selected as captain for the British and Irish Lions tour to South Africa, but with just weeks to go, he dislocated his shoulder and doctors told him that he would be out for at least three months. No way was Alun Wyn going to miss that tour! He was back in 21 days and played for the Lions in all three tests.

But behind all that rugby toughness lies a kind, friendly man. For example, before a particularly cold, wet Six Nations match against Ireland in 2019, Alun Wyn took off his Wales team jacket and wrapped it around the shivering shoulders of seven-year-old mascot Joey Hobbs. What a legend!

158 caps for Wales, four tours with the British and Irish Lions — he's Mr Indestructible! He was always an inspiration to the young players following in his footsteps.

RISING STAR

JOE McCARTHY
SECOND ROW

POSITION **SECOND ROW (LOCK)**

DATE OF BIRTH **26 MARCH 2001**

COUNTRY **IRELAND**

CLUB **LEINSTER**

SUPERSTAR MOMENT **WINNING THE 2024 SIX NATIONS WITH IRELAND**

FUN FACT **JOE WAS ACTUALLY BORN IN NEW YORK, USA, BUT HIS FAMILY MOVED BACK TO IRELAND WHEN HE WAS THREE.**

JOE McCARTHY

Joe McCarthy might be rugby's ultimate rising star. He only made his senior debut for Leinster in January 2022, but by November that year, he was already making his international debut for Ireland (against Australia)!

Aged 22, he was the youngest member of Ireland's 2023 Men's Rugby World Cup squad, starting in their first game against Romania and scoring his first international try!

By the Six Nations in February 2024, Joe was part of Ireland's starting second row. In their opening game against France, he ended up with: nine tackles, nine ball-carries, two lineouts won, plus one Player of the Match award.

A new superstar was born, and a new deadly second row partnership with Tadhg Beirne. While Beirne is the calm, experienced one, Joe is the fearless enforcer, throwing himself into every tackle and breakdown.

Joe is tough with a positive mindset. He has a bright future ahead. Who knows, he's maybe a future Ireland captain!

★ RISING STAR ★

MANAÉ FELEU
SECOND ROW

POSITION **SECOND ROW (LOCK)**

DATE OF BIRTH **3 FEBRUARY 2000**

COUNTRY **FRANCE**

CLUB **FC GRENOBLE AMAZONES**

SUPERSTAR MOMENT **BECOMING CAPTAIN OF FRANCE AT THE AGE OF 23**

FUN FACT **FRANCE HAD TWO SETS OF SISTERS IN THEIR 2024 WOMEN'S SIX NATIONS SQUAD: MANAÉ AND TEANI FELEU, AND ROMANE AND MARINE MÉNAGER.**

MANAÉ FELEU

Can you call someone a "rising star" when they're already the captain of their country? Yes, when it comes to Manaé Feleu, because she's only just getting started.

After kicking off her career in Futuna, a South Pacific Island, and then New Zealand, Manae was called up to play for her country of birth, France, at the 2021 Women's Rugby World Cup. And just two years later, aged 23, she became their youngest-ever captain!

In the 2024 Women's Six Nations, Manaé led France to four strong wins out of five, and their only defeat came in the Grand Slam decider against England. After making 51 tackles and seventeen lineout takes, fans voted her on to the official Team of the Tournament, as the stand-out player in her position. She also got to start together with her sister, Teani (a number 8), for the first time!

Manaé is a dynamic player who loves to run through people, so don't get in her way!

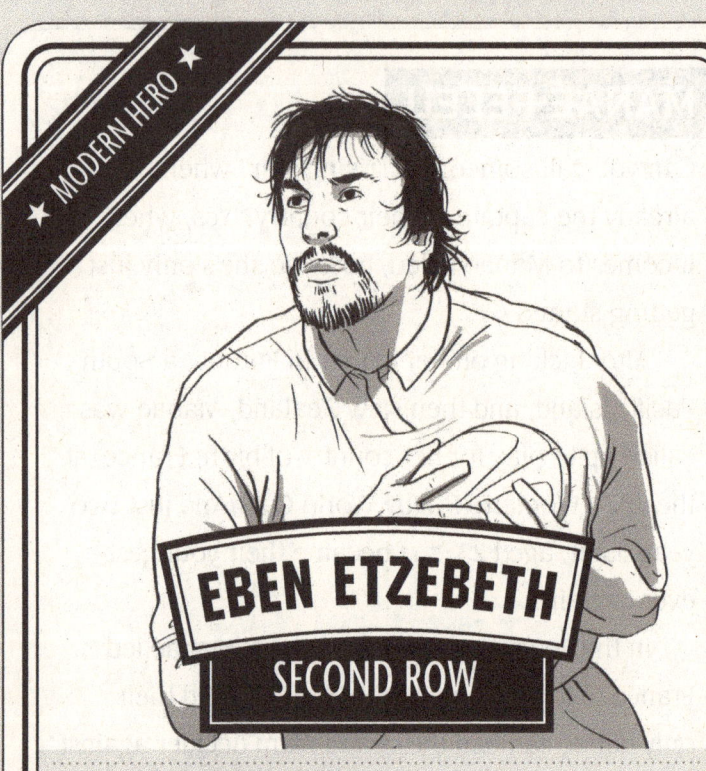

★ MODERN HERO ★

EBEN ETZEBETH
SECOND ROW

POSITION **SECOND ROW (LOCK)**

DATE OF BIRTH **29 OCTOBER 1991**

COUNTRY **SOUTH AFRICA**

CLUBS **WESTERN PROVINCE, STORMERS, RED HURRICANES OSAKA, TOULON, SHARKS**

SUPERSTAR MOMENT **WINNING BACK-TO-BACK MEN'S RUGBY WORLD CUPS IN 2019 AND 2023**

FUN FACT **WHEN EBEN WON HIS 100th TEST CAP IN JULY 2022, THERE WAS A SPECIAL GUEST TO SING THE SOUTH AFRICAN NATIONAL ANTHEM: HIS FIANCÉE (NOW WIFE) ACTRESS AND SINGER ANLIA VAN RENSBURG!**

EBEN ETZEBETH

Who is rugby's strongest superstar? Who is the player you'd least like to meet alone in a dark alley? Our answer to both of those questions would be the same second-row man-mountain: South Africa's Eben Etzebeth.

We're talking about a player who stands 2.03 metres (6 ft 8 in) tall, and weighs in at over 120 kg of pure muscle. Eben built his strength as a young player at the club, Stormers, chest-pressing with 75 kg dumbbells. That's like lifting his South Africa teammate Manie Libbok with each arm!

Eben has inherited strength, too. His dad, Harry, was a wrestler, and so was his uncle, Cliffie, who represented South Africa at a world wrestling tournament.

And Eben isn't afraid of going head-to-head with anyone. It's usually his opponents who are terrified, but even his teammates aren't always safe. When he played against his long-time South Africa second-row partner, Lood de Jager, in a club match in 2016, they ended up wrestling each other on the grass! Who won? Well, we'd say Eben, but we're too scared to say otherwise…

But Eben is usually too smart to get too carried away on the rugby pitch (especially if the referee's watching!). In his 131 appearances for South Africa, he has actually received only three yellow cards and zero red cards. Instead, Eben uses his incredible power for the good of his team! Whether he's competing in a tackle, a scrum, a ruck or a lineout, he does everything with full force and full commitment.

Eben isn't just a big, muscly battering ram, though; he's also an athlete with serious rugby skills. Growing up, he played as a back, rather than a forward, and he was also a good sprinter and high jumper. It was only after a huge growth spurt as a teenager that he moved into the second row.

Eben played for the South Africa Under-18s alongside Siya Kolisi, and then for the Under-20s at the 2011 International Rugby Board (IRB) Junior World Championship, before debuting as a senior international in 2012. It was a golden era for the South Africa second row, and so Eben got the chance to learn from two of the best – Victor Matfield and Bakkies Botha – before becoming his country's first-choice number 4 in 2014.

At the 2015 Men's Rugby World Cup, he scored a try against Argentina to secure the Bronze Medal for South Africa, but the best was yet to come. Four years later, at the 2019 tournament in Japan, his second-row partnership with de Jager helped power the Springboks to the final. Despite a shoulder injury, Eben helped South Africa to dominate the scrum and the lineout as they defeated England.

Perhaps his greatest moment, however, came in the 2023 Men's Rugby World Cup quarter-finals. With South Africa trailing 25–19, and time running out, Eben collected a pass from Faf de Klerk and – BOOM! – he powered his way past four France players to score the match-winning try. What a hero! Two gruelling games later, Eben and South Africa were World Champions again.

Eben strikes fear into the opposition whenever he plays. He is one of the world's best because as well as being really big, he is also a master of the game, and it is that expertise and knowledge that enable him to dominate.

MODERN HERO

ZOE ALDCROFT
SECOND ROW

POSITION **SECOND ROW (LOCK), FLANKER (NO. 6)**

DATE OF BIRTH **19 NOVEMBER 1996**

COUNTRY **ENGLAND**

CLUBS **DARLINGTON MOWDEN PARK SHARKS, GLOUCESTER-HARTPURY WOMEN**

SUPERSTAR MOMENT **BEING NAMED WORLD RUGBY WOMEN'S PLAYER OF THE YEAR 2021**

FUN FACT **ZOE HAS A GOOD LUCK CHARM THAT SHE CARRIES IN HER BAG TO EVERY GAME: A LITTLE DOLL OF ENGLAND LEGEND JONNY WILKINSON THAT WAS KNITTED BY HER FRIEND'S GRAN!**

ZOE ALDCROFT

Growing up in Scarborough, England, Zoe had a very busy and varied sporting schedule: rugby and netball, but also dance and ballet. It was only at the age of fifteen that she decided to focus on her favourite, and she chose ... rugby, duh!

Her older brother, Jonathan, first got her into the game when she was eight, and Zoe showed her talent for rugby straight away. After starting out in a boys' team at Scarborough RUFC, she then played for a series of local girls' teams. Then, in 2013, aged sixteen, she moved from her family home in the North-East of England all the way down to Hartpury College in the South-West. The college is famous for developing top rugby players, and it's also the home of Gloucester-Hartpury, one of the best women's teams in the country.

For the next few years, Zoe studied sport and exercise nutrition, while doing a full-time rugby programme. It was the ideal environment for her to improve as a player, and in July 2016, she was called up to the England senior team for the first time. She made her debut as a late sub against France, and within four minutes, she had scored the winning try. Talk about making an instant impact!

A year later, Zoe was part of the Red Roses squad for the 2017 Women's Rugby World Cup in Ireland, but she didn't get to play in the biggest games. It was all a good learning experience, though, and by the time the next tournament came around five years later (delayed from 2021 to 2022 due to Covid-19), Zoe was not only a regular starter in the England second row, but was the World Rugby Women's Player of the Year. In New Zealand, the Red Roses cruised through to yet another World Cup final, but again, they were beaten by the Black Ferns. It was so frustrating, especially for Zoe, who had to go off with a head injury after only 27 minutes.

Might Zoe have made the difference? She was certainly a massive loss, both for her leadership skills and her rugby skills. She is particularly amazing in the lineouts. At 1.82 metres (5 ft 11 in), she's not one of the tallest players in the women's game, and yet she's almost unbeatable in the air. At the 2024 Women's Six Nations, where England won a Grand Slam, Zoe had the most lineout takes in the whole tournament, and came second in lineout steals, too.

So, how does she do it? Well, first of all, she's a real student of the game: "I enjoy taking the time to look at another team's lineout and I love to look at the little details of our lineout."

And secondly, according to Zoe, those early years of dancing have also really helped: "I found performing in dance shows similar because you have to remember what dance you're doing and in rugby you have to remember the moves at the lineout and where you are going to be positioned."

Well, after being announced as the new England captain in January 2025, Zoe looks like she's going to keep dancing on the rugby pitch long into the future.

MAGGIE'S INSIGHTS

I presented Zoe with her World Rugby Women's Player of the Year award in 2021 and it doesn't matter what number she has on her back, she will always perform. She can play numbers four or five, or anywhere across the back row. She is down to earth and incredibly humble. She is a joy to watch and a big favourite with the fans.

GAMECHANGER

JOHN EALES
SECOND ROW

POSITION **SECOND ROW (LOCK)**

DATE OF BIRTH **27 JUNE 1970**

COUNTRY **AUSTRALIA**

CLUBS **QUEENSLAND, QUEENSLAND REDS**

SUPERSTAR MOMENT **CAPTAINING HIS COUNTRY TO RUGBY WORLD CUP GLORY IN 1999**

FUN FACT **WHEN HE WAS SEVENTEEN, JOHN SKIPPED MATHS TO GO AND WATCH ENGLAND'S 1987 MEN'S RUGBY WORLD CUP SQUAD TRAIN AT HIS SCHOOL. SO IS NOBODY PERFECT? READ ON TO DECIDE...**

JOHN EALES

This section ends with a second rower so good that his teammates nicknamed him "Nobody". Why? Because as the saying goes, "Nobody's perfect"! Yes, meet John Eales, the multi-talented man who could do it all.

By the age of twenty, he had already:

- 🏉 starred as a cricketer for the University of Queensland,
- 🏉 graduated with a degree in Psychology,
- 🏉 and played rugby for his national team.

Not bad, eh? Then a few months after his 21st birthday, he helped Australia (nicknamed the Wallabies) win the 1991 Men's Rugby World Cup!

And John wasn't just a young back-up off the bench; he started every match. Together with the more experienced Rod McCall, he formed a powerful second-row partnership that pushed Australia all the way to glory. In their group stage match against Wales, they won 28 out of the 30 lineouts together, and, in the final against England, John played an equally important part with a try-saving tackle on Rob Andrew.

John may have won the World Cup, but that was just the start of his achievements. The more he played, the better he became. In 1996, he was named the new captain of his country. Nothing was going to stop him now, not even a nightmare 43–6 defeat against New Zealand. It was Australia's worst-ever result against their local rivals, but a week later, John led his team to a comeback victory over the World Champions, South Africa.

An exciting new era had begun for Australia, and when the 1999 Men's Rugby World Cup came around, the Wallabies were flying. In a new second-row partnership with David Giffin, John pushed Australia all the way to glory again, past Wales in the quarters, South Africa in the semis, then France in the final. And this time, John also had the proud honour of lifting the gold Webb Ellis Cup himself, with his whole family watching.

But let's talk some more about John as a player: at 2 metres (6 ft 7 in) and 120 kg, he looked like your classic second rower, making him lethal in the lineout and strong in the scrum. But we're talking about the multi-talented man who could do it all:

Tackle? *Tick!*

Catch? *Tick!*

Pass? *Tick!*

Run? *Tick!* (Although John only scored two tries in his 84 caps, he did plenty of ball-carrying for his team.)

Kick? *TICK!*

Yes, John even had a brilliant right foot for a big guy! During his international career, he kicked an incredible 164 points, to be the highest-scoring forward in Test rugby history. His greatest three points of all came in 2000, during the Bledisloe Cup away against New Zealand. With seconds to go, Australia were awarded a penalty to win the game, and up stepped John to score.

A year later, in 2001, he retired from the game as officially the most capped second row in rugby history and Australia's most successful captain (from 55 Test matches), plus unofficially his country's greatest-ever player.

What made John such a special player was his ability to kick off the tee! It's rare to see any forward take penalties for their team, but a second row? It almost never happens — so, what a legend!

★ QUIZ ★

IF SOMEONE ASKED WHAT YOUR GREATEST STRENGTH WAS, WOULD YOU SAY YOU'RE A LONG-ARMED LINEOUT LEADER, A BIG, BASHING POWERHOUSE, OR EXCELLENT AT EVERYTHING?

LONG-ARMED LINEOUT LEADER

You're ...ZOE ALDCROFT! You might not be the tallest or the strongest second rower, but your long arms and brilliant rugby brain make you unbeatable in the air.

BIG, BASHING POWERHOUSE

Are you so big and angry that even your own teammates are a little scared of you?

→ YES
→ NO

EXCELLENT AT EVERYTHING

Can you even kick as well as a fly-half?

→ YES
→ NO

Do you have any brothers or sisters who really love rugby, too?

YES → You're ... MANAÉ FELEU! You're a lineout leader who can tackle, run, and pass as well, but watch out: you're not the only superstar in your family!

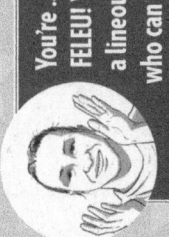

NO → You're ... ALUN WYN JONES! Solid as a rock with zero weaknesses, you're the most consistent second row superstar around.

You're ... JOHN EALES! You're the all-round genius they call "Nobody" because "Nobody's perfect"!

You're ... EBEN ETZEBETH! Warning! With your size and strength, you're like a rugby-playing monster, and you're not afraid to go head-to-head with anyone.

You're ... JOE MCCARTHY! Yes, you're a fearless enforcer, throwing yourself into every tackle and breakdown, but off the rugby field, you're actually a very friendly giant.

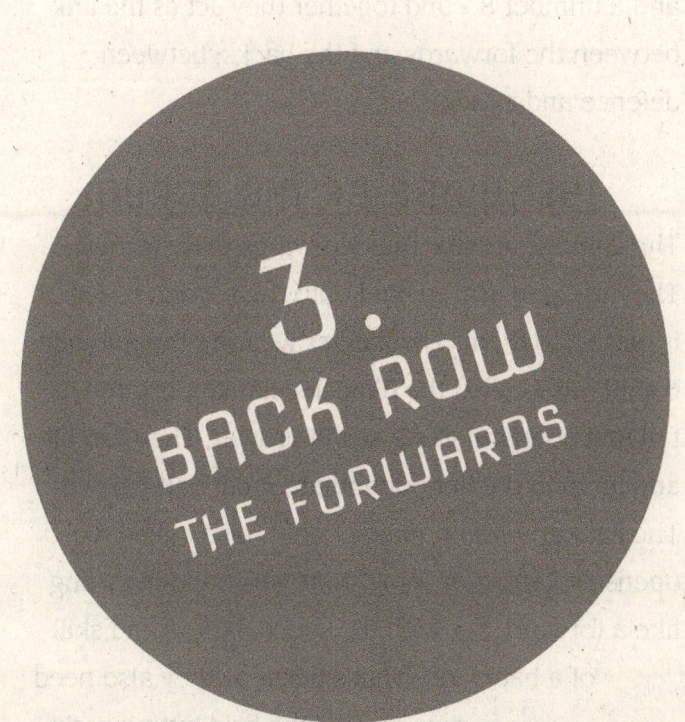

3.
BACK ROW
THE FORWARDS

We're making our way to the back of the scrum now, to meet ... the back row. The back row consists of three positions – two flankers and a number 8 – and together they act as the link between the forwards and the backs; between defence and attack.

THE WINGS OF THE SCRUM

The flankers are like the two wings of the scrum. They use one arm to bind onto the second row that is closest to them. The flanker wearing the number 6 shirt, also called the blindside flanker, is often tall and powerful like a second rower. They can lift and jump in the lineout and are great ball-carriers. The flanker in the number 7 shirt, also called the openside flanker, is more of an all-rounder: strong like a forward, but with the speed, fitness and skill of a back, too. That's because they also need to race around the field hitting rucks, making tackles, and bursting forwards on the attack.

LAST PLAYER DOWN

If the flankers are the wings of the scrum, then the number 8 is the tail. They slot in at the back of the scrum and bind onto the two second rowers and are the last player down in the scrum. They have a specific role at the scrum – to control the ball when it reaches the back of the scrum using their feet – so they tend to have very good ball control skills. During the scrum, the number 8 works very closely with the scrum-half (the number 9), to decide when the ball should be taken out of the scrum and played. Sometimes, however, it's the number 8 who takes the ball and runs with it, so they need to be powerful runners, as well as powerful tacklers.

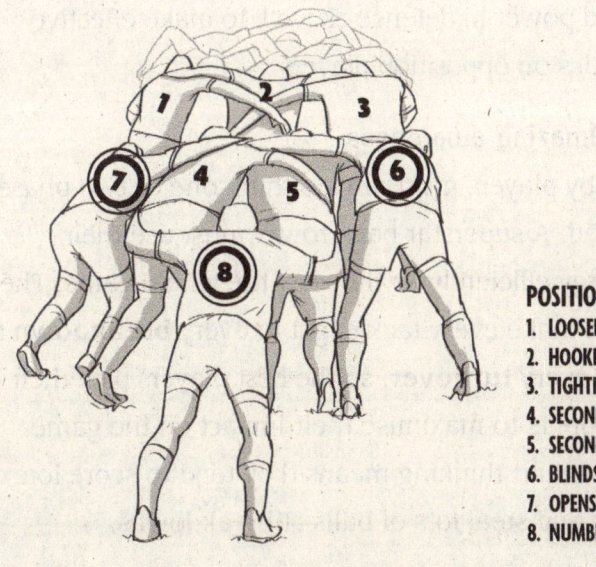

POSITION
1. LOOSEHEAD PROP
2. HOOKER
3. TIGHTHEAD PROP
4. SECOND ROW
5. SECOND ROW
6. BLINDSIDE FLANKER
7. OPENSIDE FLANKER
8. NUMBER 8

TO BE A BACK ROW SUPERSTAR YOU NEED:

1. Fantastic fitness and handling skills

Back rowers are expected to be everywhere on the pitch: attacking and defending; running, lifting, tackling and handling the ball. To do all that, all game long, they have to be some of the fittest players on the team.

2. Explosive power

Back rowers are excellent ball-carriers, so they have explosive power and a low centre of gravity to help them break through tackles and accelerate through gaps when making a clean break. They need to have good power in defence as well, to make effective tackles on opposition players.

3. Amazing awareness

Rugby players must always think one or two phases ahead. A superstar back rower must use their energy efficiently so they last the whole game. They can't make every tackle, get to every **breakdown** or win every **turnover**, so the best players pick their moments to maximise their impact on the game. This smart thinking means they tend to score lots of tries and steal lots of balls at breakdowns.

RUGBY RULES

BREAKDOWNS AND TURNOVERS

The BREAKDOWN is the period of play that comes after a player is tackled and before the ball is then picked up and passed on by a teammate. Why "breakdown"? Well, at that point, the game kind of pauses and breaks down for a bit, as everyone starts rucking or mauling!

A TURNOVER is when the ball switches from one team to the other. This often happens at the breakdown as both teams battle for the ball. Winning turnovers? Great! Conceding turnovers? Not so great. If you win a turnover, it means you've stolen the ball off the opposition and won possession back for your team. If you concede a turnover, it means you've had the ball stolen off you by the opposition and you've lost possession for your team.

LEADING FROM THE BACK

Back rowers have to be all-action performers. They're at the centre of everything – defence and attack – and therefore in the perfect position to captain a team. That's why so many of the greatest rugby leaders of all time have been back rowers, including:

FACTS

- **Francois Pienaar**, who inspired South Africa to victory at the 1995 Men's Rugby World Cup, helping to unite the racially-divided nation alongside president Nelson Mandela.
- **Sarah Hunter**, England's most capped player of all time, and the captain when the Red Roses won the 2014 Women's Rugby World Cup.
- New Zealand's **Richie McCaw** (2011 and 2015) and South Africa's **Siya Kolisi** (2019 and 2023), the only two captains to win two Men's Rugby World Cups (more on them in a few pages!).
- **Gaëlle Hermet**, who led France to a Women's Six Nations Grand Slam in 2018, and then a Bronze Medal finish at the 2021 Women's Rugby World Cup.

THE BACK ROW THEN ...

In the old days, the first and most important job of the back row was to defend. Their aim was to tackle and race into every breakdown to try and win turnovers.

... V. THE BACK ROW NOW

These days, back row players tend to have better ball skills and do more attacking. Sure, they still have to do all the defensive dirty work, but with their winning mix of speed and strength, they can have a huge impact on both sides of the ball.

SO, WHICH KIND OF BACK ROWER WOULD YOU BE?

What sounds more fun: attacking, defending, or lots of both? Will you be best known for your ball-carrying, or your battling work at the breakdown? Or maybe you'll be the ultimate back row all-rounder!

To help you decide, here's a look at some of the most brilliant back rowers rugby has ever seen, all with different styles and approaches. Then take our quiz to find out which superstar you would be.

★ LEGEND ★

RICHIE McCAW
BACK ROW

POSITION **FLANKER OR NO. 8**

DATE OF BIRTH **31 DECEMBER 1980**

COUNTRY **NEW ZEALAND**

CLUBS **CANTERBURY, CRUSADERS**

SUPERSTAR MOMENT **LEADING NEW ZEALAND TO BACK-TO-BACK MEN'S RUGBY WORLD CUP TITLES IN 2011 AND 2015**

FUN FACT **AFTER RETIRING FROM RUGBY, RICHIE MOVED FROM ONE OF HIS DREAM JOBS TO ANOTHER: FLYING GLIDERS AND HELICOPTERS!**

RICHIE McCAW

Don't be fooled by his nickname; the only thing "Fluffy" about Richie McCaw is his hair. Rugby legends don't get any bigger or tougher than this man. Not only was he the first All Black to reach 100 caps, and the first rugby union player to win 100 Test matches, but when he retired in 2015, Richie was also the most-capped international male player, and the flanker with the most Test tries.

Not bad for a boy who only started taking rugby seriously aged fourteen! Richie grew up on a farm on New Zealand's South Island, flying glider planes with his grandfather, and playing for his local club, Kurow. It was only at Otago Boys' High School that Richie really stood out, and after winning the 1999 Under-19 World Rugby Championship, he thought maybe he could become an All Black...

Two years later, his dream came true. Richie was thrown in at the deep end of international rugby, in Dublin against Ireland – so, would he sink or swim? Swim, of course, all the way to the top! By 2004, Richie had been named New Zealand captain and by 2006, he had won the first of his three World Rugby Men's Player of the Year awards.

And what about the World Cup? Well, Richie's first two tournaments ended in big disappointment, with defeats in the semi-finals in 2003, then the quarter-finals in 2007. Woah, were the All Blacks losing their golden touch?

No – captain Richie was going to lead his country back to greatness. Despite fracturing his foot, nothing was going to stop him or his New Zealand team at the 2011 Men's Rugby World Cup. They stormed past Argentina and then Australia, to set up a final against France, the team that had beaten them in 2007. Oooo, it was time for revenge, and boy, did it taste sweet, especially for Richie, who lifted the Webb Ellis Cup high into the Auckland sky. He was a World Champion at last!

And four years later, in the last of his 148 international matches, Richie got to do it all over again. In the 2015 final, New Zealand beat Australia 34–17 to become the first team to win back-to-back World Cups. Wow, what a way to say goodbye!

Former New Zealand coach Graham Henry called him "the best leader this country has ever had", but what was Richie like as an actual player? Well, he was everything you'd want from a world-class flanker, especially in those days: energetic, consistent, powerful, tough in the tackle, relentless at rucks, great at reading the game, and the best in the world at winning turnovers. Richie's opponents didn't always like the way he tested the rules and referees, but his teammates and his country certainly did. In 2016, he was even appointed as one of only twenty living members of the Order of New Zealand.

MAGGIE'S INSIGHTS

I first met Richie in 2006, when I won the Women's Player of the Year award and he won Men's Player of the Year. What made it special was that we were both openside flankers at the top of our game. He shook my hand and introduced himself (even though I already knew who he was) and we had a really normal conversation about rugby, as if we had known each other for years.

★ RISING STAR ★

AOIFE WAFER
BACK ROW

POSITION **FLANKER OR NO. 8**

DATE OF BIRTH **25 MARCH 2003**

COUNTRY **IRELAND**

CLUBS **LEINSTER**

SUPERSTAR MOMENT **WINNING THE 2024 GUINNESS RUGBY WRITERS OF IRELAND WOMEN'S PLAYER OF THE YEAR AWARD**

FUN FACT **AOIFE'S YOUNGER SISTER, ORLA, IS ALSO A RISING STAR WITH THE IRELAND UNDER-20S.**

AOIFE WAFER

It all started for Aoife Wafer at the age of six, when her older brothers began playing at Gorey FC, their local rugby club in County Wexford, Ireland.

"I of course was left in the clubhouse and I just wanted to get stuck in," Aoife explains. "I wanted to be out with the boys and I wanted to play. So one day [my mum] let me go out, and I didn't really look back."

Aoife started out as a scrum-half ("I was really bossy and I was really small"), but after a growth spurt, her coaches at Enniscorthy RFC decided to move her into the back row. With her power, speed and perseverance, flanker turned out to be the perfect fit. Soon, she was playing for Leinster and captaining the Ireland Under-18s.

What next – playing for the Ireland senior team? No, first Aoife decided to join the Ireland Rugby Sevens programme, where she continued to develop her game. "I honestly don't think I would be in the position I am in today if I hadn't had sevens experience," she says. "It just puts such a focus on your core, basic skills – your catch, your pass, your tackle, everything."

But eventually, the senior Ireland rugby team came calling. Aged nineteen, Aoife won her first cap in the 2022 Women's Six Nations against Italy, and what a strange debut it turned out to be. "I got on the pitch, got a yellow card and came off the pitch" – she tells the short story – "I got back on the pitch, got a turnover, and then the match was done."

Oh well, Aoife would have plenty more chances to play for Ireland ... or would she? Due to injuries, she missed the rest of the 2022 tournament, and then the whole of the 2023 tournament! Would Ireland's rising star ever return?

Yes! With the support of her teammates, Aoife came battling back in time for the 2024 Women's Six Nations. For Ireland's first game against France, she was even picked to start alongside her hero, captain and fellow flanker Edel McMahon. And the result? Wearing her trademark red scrum cap, Aoife was amazing, especially with the ball in hand. She made seventeen carries, two offloads, and she even beat two defenders to score her first international try.

There was even better to come a few weeks later in Ireland's third match against Wales.

Catching the ball wide on the left wing, Aoife dummied a pass and then charged her way to the try line again, this time powering past three opponents.

She also earned a place in the Team of the Tournament, plus the 2024 Guinness Rugby Writers of Ireland Women's Player of the Year award, too. A year later, Aoife kicked off the 2025 Six Nations tournament with two more tries in Ireland's opening game against France, and the most incredible thing? She's still only 22! So, watch out for that red scrum cap – Aoife's on her way to the top of world rugby, and there's no stopping her now.

One of the standout players during the 2024 Women's Six Nations, Aoife is a role model to many who face adversity and never give up.

★ MODERN HERO ★

PIETER-STEPH DU TOIT

BACK ROW

POSITION **FLANKER (NO. 7)**

DATE OF BIRTH **20 AUGUST 1992**

COUNTRY **SOUTH AFRICA**

CLUBS **SHARKS, STORMERS, TOYOTA VERBLITZ**

SUPERSTAR MOMENT **WINNING PLAYER OF THE MATCH IN THE 2023 MEN'S RUGBY WORLD CUP FINAL**

FUN FACT **HE'S THE SEVENTH "PIETER-STEPH DU TOIT" IN HIS FAMILY, AND GUESS WHAT HE CALLED HIS SON! YEP, "PIETER-STEPH" TOO!**

PIETER-STEPH DU TOIT

"I want to be spoken about as a great of the game," Pieter-Steph du Toit said back in 2021. Well, congratulations – with two World Cup wins and two World Rugby Men's Player of the Year awards, you've already achieved your goal!

But let's go back to the beginning. One day, Pieter-Steph and his younger brother Johan were at home in Cape Town, South Africa, when they made a discovery: some old rugby photographs, an old rugby shirt and boots. Interesting! Who did they belong to? The answer was their grandfather, Piet du Toit, who played as a prop for South Africa in the late 1950s and early 1960s. For both brothers, a dream was born that day...

Pieter-Steph began his career as a flanker, but by high school, his coaches were telling him that he had grown too big! At 1.98 metres (6 ft 6 in) tall and weighing over 114 kg, he was a successful second row lock for his club, the Sharks, and for his country too. Pieter-Steph made his South Africa debut in 2013, but in 2016, he switched to play as a flanker instead. At first, Pieter-Steph struggled back in his old position at international level, but with the help of new coach Rassie Erasmus, he turned himself into one of the best flankers in the world.

How? Well, with lots of hard work, Pieter-Steph was able to combine the strength and size of a second rower in the scrum and the lineout with the speed and skill of a back rower at the breakdown. That already sounds like a pretty amazing mix, doesn't it, and we haven't even got on to Pieter-Steph's two greatest weapons:

1. His resilience

In 2014, he tore the ACL, an important ligament in his knee, which put him out of action, and then a year later, he tore it again. Uh-oh, surely Pieter-Steph would have to miss the 2015 Men's Rugby World Cup? No way! His dad donated a hamstring tendon, which was inserted into his knee as his new ACL and Pieter-Steph rushed back to play!

Then in 2020, he almost lost his leg after two bad hits in one match caused a major medical emergency. Would Pieter-Steph ever be able to play rugby again? Oh yes, he came battling back in time to beat the British and Irish Lions in 2021!

2. His tackling

With his long arms and excellent technique, Pieter-Steph is almost impossible to get past. He played a crucial part in the 2019 Men's Rugby World Cup final as South Africa overpowered England, and in the 2023 final, he was even better, making an astonishing 28 tackles against New Zealand. Yes, you heard that right – 28 tackles in one single match! So, there you go – Pieter-Steph du Toit, a true great of the game already, and his brother's dream worked out pretty well, too. Johan has played for the Stormers for the last seven years, four of those alongside Pieter-Steph. Awww, their grandfather would be very proud.

MAGGIE'S INSIGHTS

I had the privilege of being at the 2023 Men's Rugby World Cup final when South Africa won the title for the second time, and I was honoured to present Pieter-Steph with his Player of the Match award. As a fellow back-rower, I love watching him play and the strength and work-rate he brings to the game.

MODERN HERO

GRÉGORY ALLDRITT

BACK ROW

POSITION **NO. 8**

DATE OF BIRTH **23 MARCH 1997**

COUNTRY **FRANCE**

CLUBS **AUCH, LA ROCHELLE**

SUPERSTAR MOMENT **WINNING THE SIX NATIONS GRAND SLAM IN 2022**

FUN FACT **DUE TO HIS DIVERSE FAMILY BACKGROUND, GRÉGORY COULD ALSO HAVE PLAYED RUGBY FOR: IRELAND, ITALY, DENMARK, OR KENYA!**

GRÉGORY ALLDRITT

It's time to look at a true number 8 at the top of the modern game. Not that Grégory Alldritt would say that about himself; he's far too modest and humble. "I am lucky enough to get up in the morning to play rugby," he says. "I don't ask for anything more and I don't hope for anything better... I am living the dream and I appreciate it every day."

As a kid growing up in Toulouse, however, Grégory didn't really have a professional rugby dream. Being paid to play the game he loved at the highest level? That seemed way too good to be true! "Greg always loved rugby," says his dad, Terence. "But we didn't know he was going to be this good."

Yes, when he entered the world of professional rugby in 2016, Grégory was far from a stand-out player. At his first club, Auch, he was often in the second XV, and when he moved to La Rochelle in 2017, he started off in the development team.

But when he watched his friends from Auch, Antoine Dupont and Anthony Jelonch, shining at the top level, Grégory's hunger grew. If he worked hard enough, why couldn't he be doing that too?

When the 2018–19 Top 14 season began, Grégory was ready to make his big breakthrough. At 1.9 metres (6 ft 3 in) and 115 kg, he was already a powerful defender, but now after lots of practice, he was also a speedy, skilful attacker.

Ta-da! By February 2019, Grégory was making his debut for France in the Six Nations, and in his third game, he scored two late tries to beat Scotland.

The first was a classic piece of number 8 play – at the back of a driving scrum, Grégory pushed and pushed, kicking the ball along with him, until the time was right to pick it up and dive over the try line. And the second? That was just pure power! By the end of the 2019 Six Nations, Grégory had forced his way into the France starting line-up and he's stayed there ever since, getting better and better.

The partnership between the number 8 and the number 9, the scrum-half, is an important part of any rugby team, and in Alldritt and Dupont, France are fortunate to have two guys who are old friends as well as super-talented players. Together, they have led their team to some amazing achievements:

- Beating Ireland in 2020, when Grégory won Player of the Match,

- Beating New Zealand in 2021, for the first time since 2009, with Grégory making 13 tackles and lots of ball-carries,
- And best of all, winning the Six Nations Grand Slam in 2022.

While Antoine picked up the Player of the Tournament award for the 2022 Six Nations, Grégory wasn't far behind. He won Player of the Match against Ireland again and he was excellent against England too, setting up a try for Antoine with a beautiful offload on the run.

When Dupont decided to skip the 2024 Six Nations to focus on the Olympic Sevens instead, the choice of France's next captain was clear: Grégory. And a year later, when Dupont got injured ahead of their crucial final game against Scotland, Grégory stepped in again to lead France to the 2025 Six Nation's title.

MAGGIE'S INSIGHTS

I love watching Grégory. I never played number 8, but if I did, I would have modelled myself on the way he plays. He's a mean tackler, an accurate passer and a knowledgeable player who can read the game brilliantly.

★ MODERN HERO ★

ALEX MATTHEWS
BACK ROW

POSITION **FLANKER OR NO. 8**

DATE OF BIRTH **3 AUGUST 1993**

COUNTRY **ENGLAND**

CLUBS **WORCESTER WARRIORS, GLOUCESTER-HARTPURY**

SUPERSTAR MOMENT **WINNING 2024 ENGLAND WOMEN'S PLAYER OF THE YEAR**

FUN FACT **HER ELDER SISTER, FRAN, IS A WINGER WHO ALSO REPRESENTED ENGLAND AT RUGBY. THEY PLAYED TOGETHER FOR THE FIRST TIME IN 2012.**

ALEX MATTHEWS

The first part of Alex Matthews' long and amazing rugby career was like a fairy tale. After starting out at Camberley RFC in Surrey aged three, Alex made her England debut in 2011, aged seventeen, and then aged just 21, she won the 2014 Women's Rugby World Cup.

Wow, what an achievement! At that time, Alex was still a back-up for England's first-choice flankers, but she came on for the last fifteen minutes of the final against Canada to claim her winner's medal.

What next? Well, the middle part of Alex's journey was a real mix of highs and lows, as she spent the next eight years bouncing back and forth between her two favourite games:

1. **Rugby sevens** – She helped Team GB win a Bronze Medal at the 2018 Commonwealth Games, but then experienced the disappointment of losing the Bronze Medal match at the 2020 Olympic Games (delayed from 2020 to 2021 due to Covid-19).
2. **Rugby union** – She was part of the Red Roses team that won six Women's Six

Nations titles in a row (2019–24), but lost the Women's Rugby World Cup finals to New Zealand in 2017 and 2021.

And important defeats weren't the only frustration for Alex. Early in her career, she had to work part-time as a carer to earn extra money. Then, when the Team GB rugby sevens funding was suddenly cut, she had to find another way to train and pay for the trip to the 2020 Olympic Games.

So, Alex spent the season playing rugby union for Worcester Warriors, and she enjoyed the experience so much that in 2023, she signed permanently for Gloucester-Hartpury, which turned out to be the start of an exciting new era. Not only has Alex won two Premiership Women's Rugby league titles with her club, but she's also performing better than ever for her country, and in a new role, too.

"Being a back row [for me] is the best position," she says, "because you get to be sort of as dynamic and as fast as some of the backs, but then you've got to be as strong and powerful as the forwards." But after years as a flanker, she moved to number 8 in 2023, when captain Sarah Hunter retired.

What a successful switch it's been! Alex still makes full use of her pace and power to hit the rucks hard, but she also has more time and space to make smart attacking runs. During the 2023 Women's Six Nations, she scored two late tries against Ireland in one match, and then broke off the back of the scrum to add another against France.

Then, at the next Women's Six Nations, Alex scored two crucial tries against France to earn another Grand Slam for her country, as well as the 2024 England Women's Player of the Year award for herself.

But despite all her individual and team success, Alex is focused on creating a bright future for English women's rugby. "The atmosphere, the feel, the crowd that we bring in" are what matters most to her. "We want to inspire."

Words can't fully describe just how talented Alex is. She's committed to being a master of her craft. I used to coach her in her youth, and even back then, she showed a real desire to be the best.

★ ENTERTAINER ★

ARDIE SAVEA
BACK ROW

POSITION **FLANKER OR NO. 8**

DATE OF BIRTH **14 OCTOBER 1993**

COUNTRY **NEW ZEALAND**

CLUBS **WELLINGTON, HURRICANES, KOBELCO KOBE STEELERS, MOANA PASIFIKA**

SUPERSTAR MOMENT **BEING NAMED 2023 WORLD RUGBY MEN'S PLAYER OF THE YEAR**

FUN FACT **IN 2019, HE BECAME THE FIRST RUGBY PLAYER TO WEAR GOGGLES AT THE MEN'S RUGBY WORLD CUP AGAINST CANADA.**

ARDIE SAVEA

Looking for a back rower who really can do it all? Then Ardie Savea is your man. This is a guy so multi-talented that at college he:

- performed in the musical *Joseph and the Amazing Technicolor Dreamcoat*,
- ran the 100 metres in 11.4 seconds,
- AND starred for the rugby team!

Across nearly 100 caps for New Zealand, he has switched between the number 6, 7, and 8 shirts so often that many aren't sure what his best position actually is. Ardie has his favourite, though.

"I think going to eight has suited my skill set," he said in 2023. "When I was a seven, coming through the ranks, I got told to clean rucks, work-horse, engine, which is the Richie McCaw model, and that wasn't me."

No, as much as Ardie enjoys a tackle and a turn-over, what he really loves is getting his hands on the ball and attacking at every opportunity. He's the best back rower in the world at that.

Growing up in Wellington, Ardie actually started out as a back, like his brother and fellow All Black,

Julian. But while Julian stayed as a winger, Ardie ended up moving from centre to the back row. And guess what! He was great at it!

Instead of settling straight into an international rugby career, however, Ardie spent three years playing rugby sevens for New Zealand. All that quick running, passing, thinking and tackling meant that by the time he finally made his All Blacks debut in 2016, his all-round game was ridiculous! "Ardie is a freak," says his teammate, TJ Perenara. "He can do some things on the field that no one else can do."

At first, Ardie was used as an explosive super-sub. But in September 2016, he started alongside Julian against South Africa, and they became the first brothers to both score tries in the same game for New Zealand!

Ardie had arrived on the world rugby stage, and the more he played, the better and more entertaining he became. More devastating dummies, more outrageous offloads, and more rampaging runs. "If you can stop me, you stop me," he warns. "But I'm going to fight through it."

The only thing missing? A World Cup trophy.

In the semi-final against England in 2019, Ardie did his best to spark a comeback with a second-half try, but it ended in defeat for the All Blacks. Four years later, he scored to lead New Zealand past Ireland in the quarter-finals, but they couldn't quite power past South Africa in the final.

Oh well, for now, Ardie will just have to make do with the 2023 World Rugby Men's Player of the Year award, and move on, which is yet another thing that he's great at. "I train, I play, I do my analysis and after that, no rugby," he says. But if he keeps training and playing so well, he could get one last shot at World Cup glory in 2027.

MAGGIE'S INSIGHTS

Ardie isn't just an entertainer, he is also a legend, a gamechanger and a modern hero, too! I was at the World Rugby Awards in 2023 when he collected the Men's Player of the Year award, and what I noticed was just how modest he was. When being interviewed on the stage, he refused to make it about him and just praised the efforts of his team. He is a real team player.

GAMECHANGER

SIYA KOLISI
BACK ROW

POSITION **FLANKER (NO. 6)**

DATE OF BIRTH **16 JUNE 1991**

COUNTRY **SOUTH AFRICA**

CLUBS **WESTERN PROVINCE, STORMERS, SHARKS, RACING 92**

SUPERSTAR MOMENT **LEADING SOUTH AFRICA TO BACK-TO-BACK MEN'S RUGBY WORLD CUP TITLES IN 2019 AND 2023**

FUN FACT **HE'S A BIG FAN OF LIVERPOOL FOOTBALL CLUB. "I TRIED FOOTBALL, BUT I WASN'T SO GOOD," HE SAYS. "I COULDN'T KICK STRAIGHT, SO I MOVED TO RUGBY."**

SIYA KOLISI

Growing up in Port Elizabeth, South Africa, Siya's young life was full of heartbreak and hardship. "It's tough to stay on the right path," he says, looking back, "because sometimes hunger makes you do things that you never thought you would do."

Siya first began playing rugby for a local team aged seven, and after impressing in a youth tournament, he was offered a scholarship for Grey High School, one of the best sporting schools in South Africa.

When Siya arrived there, aged twelve, he worked hard to adapt to his new environment. He was determined to make the most of his opportunity, and watching South Africa win the 2007 Men's Rugby World Cup gave him even more motivation.

By the age of 21, Siya was already a senior international, but becoming a regular starter was going to be a much greater challenge. At the 2015 Men's Rugby World Cup, Siya only came off the bench in a few of the group games, but by the 2017 Rugby Championship, he had forced his way into the starting XV, and a year later, he was the new national team captain! And not just that; Siya was South Africa's first-ever Black rugby captain.

Why is that so significant? Because of apartheid in South Africa, a racist system that meant that between 1948 and 1991, by law, white South Africans had more rights and powers than Black people. In 1981, Errol Tobias became the first Black player to play for South Africa, but when the Springboks won the Men's Rugby World Cup fourteen years later, there was still only one Black player in the team, Chester Williams. So for South Africa to now have a Black player as the captain of their national team? Wow, that was a massive moment.

And what a brilliant and inspiring leader he has turned out to be for the Springboks. First, he captained his country to World Cup glory in 2019, and then four years later, he did it again, despite suffering a serious knee injury only a few months before the tournament!

As a flanker, Siya brings lots of power and energy to the South Africa pack. Earlier in his career, he was more of an attacking ball-carrier, but these days, he does more of the dirty work too, winning lots of tackles and turnovers for the team. Former England player, Will Greenwood, is probably right, though: "Kolisi is not the star player. He might not be the first player that you put down on the teamsheet. But as a leader he is just incredible."

And Siya's influence goes far beyond the rugby pitch. His Kolisi Foundation works in South Africa's poorest communities to tackle inequality and help provide food, education, and sports programmes. "I'm not only trying to inspire Black kids but people from all races," he said back in 2018. "We as players represent the whole country… We represent something much bigger than we can imagine."

MAGGIE'S INSIGHTS

Siya is the humblest person I have ever met in rugby. What I most admire about him is his ability to be a role model to many, regardless of gender, race and background. His story and achievements are testament that you should never give up and your start does not have to define you.

★ GAMECHANGER ★

SOPHIE DE GOEDE

BACK ROW

POSITION **NO. 8**

DATE OF BIRTH **30 JUNE 1999**

COUNTRY **CANADA**

CLUB **SARACENS**

SUPERSTAR MOMENT **LEADING CANADA TO THE 2021 WOMEN'S RUGBY WORLD CUP SEMI-FINALS**

FUN FACT **THE THING SOPHIE MISSES MOST WHEN SHE'S IN ENGLAND? "IT'S REALLY HARD TO FIND GOOD MAPLE SYRUP HERE!"**

SOPHIE DE GOEDE

How does a kid from Canada, the land of ice hockey, end up playing rugby? It's a good question, and growing up on Vancouver Island, Sophie de Goede certainly tried a lot of other sports, too: basketball, football (the "soccer" kind), volleyball, field hockey, swimming, rowing, cross-country…

But no, rugby was the sport that Sophie chose. Why? Well, her dad, Hans de Goede, was the captain of Canada's men's rugby team and her mum, Stephanie White, was the first-ever captain of the women's team. So, what choice did Sophie have?!

"My earliest memories are running around on the rugby pitch while my parents were coaching," she says, "a doll in one hand and a rugby ball in the other."

Sophie was soon hooked and inspired to follow in the footsteps of her parents, but also the Canadian heroes she grew up watching: the team that reached the semi-finals of the 2006 Women's Rugby World Cup, and the team that made it all the way to the final in 2014. One day, she dreamed, she would be out there playing too.

After school, Sophie carried on playing rugby

at Queen's University in Ontario. But when their season was cancelled due to Covid-19, she made a big life decision: to move to London and join Saracens instead!

That season in English rugby was an amazing experience for Sophie, and she returned to Canada feeling even more determined to pursue her sporting dreams. In 2021–22, not only did she lead the Queen's University women's rugby team to their first championship, but she also helped the women's basketball team to win a bronze medal!

Next up: the Women's Rugby World Cup in New Zealand in 2022. Sophie was delighted to be selected for the Canada squad, and there was more exciting news to follow – she had also been named as the new national team captain, at the age of 23! Wow, what an honour, and what a World Cup it turned out to be. Canada made it all the way to the semi-finals, and their young leader? She became a superstar.

Like our other back row gamechanger, Ardie Savea, Sophie can do it all on the rugby pitch, plus she has one extra talent: kicking!

Yes, inspired by Dan Carter, Handré Pollard and Canada's own Magali Harvey, Sophie played fly-half as a kid and taught herself how to kick from YouTube videos. So at the World Cup, when she wasn't flying into tackles or breaking away on the attack, she was kicking conversions! Her success rate was 11 out of 18, which is not bad for a back row, eh?!

Sadly, Sophie suffered a bad knee injury in July 2024, but she'll be back and no doubt better than ever.

MAGGIE'S INSIGHTS

In the modern era, it's quite rare to see a top international forward who can goal-kick off the tee successfully as it's normally a back's job. Sophie is living proof that the number on your shirt does not have to define you. She's an incredible athlete and a true gamechanger.

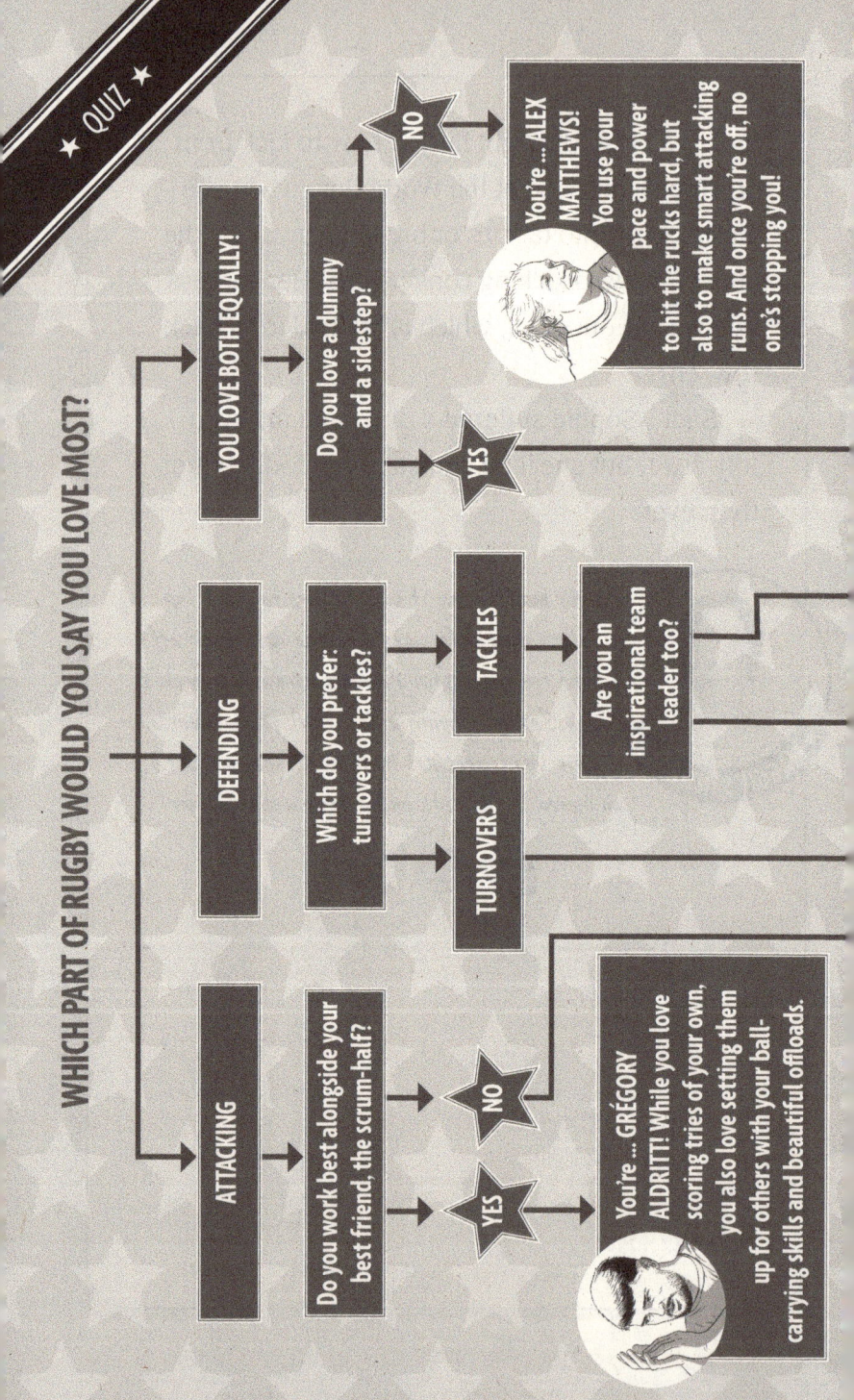

How good is your kicking?

- **NOT BAD** →

You're ... AOIFE WAFER! You don't mind defending, but your favourite thing is getting the ball, bashing your way past a few opponents, and diving over the try line.

- **BRILLIANT** →

You're ... SOPHIE DE GOEDE! What a rugby all-rounder! When you're not flying into tackles or breaking away on the attack, you're kicking conversions for your team.

- **SOMETIMES** →

You're ... RICHIE McCAW! Relentless at rucks, you're great at reading the game and staying on the right side of the referee, which is crucial when it comes to winning lots of turnovers for your team.

- **ALWAYS!** →

You're ... PIETER-STEPH DU TOIT! Backs, beware! With your long arms and excellent tackling technique, you're almost impossible to get past.

You're ... ARDIE SAVEA! As much as you love a tackle and a turnover, you also want to attack at every opportunity, showing off your outrageous skills.

You're ... SIYA KOLISI! In defence, you bring lots of power and energy to your team, but it's as a captain that you shine the brightest.

4. SCRUM-HALF
THE BACKS

From the big beasts in the scrum, we're moving on to look at the slightly less muscly superstars who stand on the outside, waiting for the battle to end and the ball to emerge. This player wears the number 9 on their backs, and we call them ... the scrum-half.

THE VOCAL PASS-MASTERS

The scrum-half is there at the breakdown to collect the ball and keep the attack going. Whenever one of their teammates is tackled to the ground and has to release the ball, it's the scrum-half's task to grab it and pass (always backwards, remember – if a pass goes forwards, it's a scrum to the other team!), to get their team moving towards that try line.

The scrum-half is the crucial link between the forwards and backs. They boss the forwards around at scrums, lineouts and breakdowns, telling them where to go and when to get out of the way and give them the ball. They also have a really close relationship with the players either side of them. They talk to the number 8, in order to understand what the forwards are planning to do, and the number 10, to understand what the backs are planning to do.

So if you've got quick hands AND a quick tongue, scrum-half is the position for you!

TO BE A SCRUM-HALF SUPERSTAR YOU NEED:

1. Perfect passing

Scrum-halves do lots of passing: short passes, long passes, pop passes, spin passes, dive passes. You need to be able to pass off both hands, off the ground AND in the air, and pick out teammates who are both moving and not moving. Each and every pass needs to be 100 per cent ACCURATE, of course!

2. Incredible communication skills

The best scrum-halves never stop talking! Whether your team is in attack or defence, at a scrum or in a lineout, you always have a message to deliver: telling the backs what the forwards are going to do, and telling the forwards what the backs are going to do. Scrum-halves also have to be good listeners because they have to quickly pass on the information they hear to keep the team organized.

3. Amazing agility

A scrum-half has to be quick. In defence, they race back to catch an opponent who's broken through. In attack, they have the agility to escape from tackles and find space around a breakdown.

SMALL BUT MIGHTY

In order to be so quick and agile, scrum-halves are often the smallest players on the pitch.

FACTS

- **Riaan Jantjies**, who played scrum-half for Namibia at the 1999 Men's Rugby World Cup, stands at 1.57 metres (5 ft 2 in) tall. He's thought to be the smallest men's international player of all time.
- Japan's **Megumi Abe** is 1.47 metres (4 ft 9 in) tall, but her size doesn't stop her. "Because I'm smaller than everyone else, brushing up on skills in certain areas of my game has always been a priority for me," she says.

TO PASS OR NOT TO PASS?

While the scrum-half's main job is still to move the ball on quickly to the bigger, more powerful, and often faster players around them, it always helps if they can join the attack and score a few sneaky tries themselves.

STATS

- South Africa's **Joost van der Westhuizen** touched down 38 times during his international career (1993–2003), the men's record for a scrum-half.

- Wales' **Gareth Davies**, meanwhile, holds the men's record for the most Men's Rugby World Cup tries by a scrum-half. He crossed the line five times during the tournament in 2015, then twice in 2019, and once more in 2023.
- New Zealand's **Kendra Cocksedge** scored a crucial try in the 2017 Women's Rugby World Cup final against England AND she also kicked three conversions!
- At the 2022 Women's Six Nations, France scrum-half **Laure Sansus** scored six tries, the most in the whole tournament.

THE SCRUM-HALF THEN ...

In the old days, the scrum-half's main role was to get the ball from the forwards and give it to the backs. So, they were usually found on the edges of the rough rugby action, ready and waiting to play a quick, clever pass to the fly-half, who was the real playmaker of the team.

... V. THE SCRUM-HALF NOW

These days, however, a scrum-half has to be more of an all-round, all-action player: tackling, carrying, and in particular, kicking. Yes, they have to be excellent with their feet as well as their hands, thanks to the growing role of the box kick. That's when a player picks the ball up from a ruck or maul, and instead of playing a risky pass, they boot it away, high and far, to clear the danger but also to get their team forwards up the field.

Why is it called a box kick? Because there is a "box" on the pitch that scrum-halves are aiming for: near the touchline, and behind the front line of the other team's defence. As well as accuracy, speed is also very important because scrum-halves have only a split-second to get their kick away before it's charged down by a big, tall, long-armed opponent.

SO, WHICH KIND OF SCRUM-HALF WOULD YOU BE?

Will you be the ultimate pass-master, or will you dart towards the try line yourself? Will you be a bossy loudmouth on the pitch, or let your slick hands do the talking instead?

To help you decide, here's a look at some of the best scrum-halves rugby has ever seen, all with different styles and approaches. Then take our quiz to find out which superstar you would be.

LEGEND

GARETH EDWARDS
SCRUM-HALF

POSITION **SCRUM-HALF**

DATE OF BIRTH **12 JULY 1947**

COUNTRY **WALES**

CLUBS **CARDIFF**

SUPERSTAR MOMENT **"THAT TRY" FOR THE BARBARIANS AGAINST NEW ZEALAND**

FUN FACT **GARETH'S OTHER GREAT PASSION IS FISHING AND HE'S CAUGHT SOME WHOPPERS, INCLUDING ONE OF THE BIGGEST PIKES EVER CAUGHT IN BRITAIN!**

GARETH EDWARDS

Gareth Edwards isn't just one of the greatest scrum-halves of all time, he's also one of the greatest overall rugby players of all time.

Growing up in a small village in South Wales, Gareth was brilliant at all sports: rugby, of course, but also gymnastics, athletics (he was a Welsh Schools champion in the hurdles and the long jump), and football. When he was offered a contract by the biggest local club, Swansea Town, at the age of sixteen, it looked like football was about to win. But no, Gareth's school PE teacher, Bill Samuel, was sure that rugby was the sport for him.

The only problem? Gareth's size. He wanted to be an exciting centre, but as he was still only 1.6 metres (5 ft 3 in) tall, that wasn't going to work. "Why don't you become a scrum-half instead," Samuel suggested. Surely the role would suit a small, speedy, skilful player like him a lot better?

In his new position, Gareth won a sixth-form scholarship to Millfield, one of the best sports schools in England, and the rest is rugby history.

- **Aged 19**, Gareth made his Wales debut against France.
- **Aged 20**, he became his country's youngest-ever captain.
- **Aged 23**, Gareth played every game for the British and Irish Lions as they beat New Zealand.
- **Aged 24**, he scored one of the greatest solo tries in the history of the game, chasing down his own kick in the mud against Scotland.
- **Aged 25**, he scored a try so sensational and so famous that rugby fans simply call it "that try".

On 27 January 1973, Gareth was playing for the Barbarians (a special super team made up of the best players from all over the world, but at that time, mostly Wales!), against the mighty All Blacks at Cardiff Arms Park. "That try" was a brilliant team move involving six passes and seven different players, but it was Edwards who burst forwards from deep to finish it off in style.

Five years later, Gareth retired from the game in style too, by winning his third Six Nations Grand Slam in the last of his 53 matches in a row for Wales. What a legend!

While Gareth clearly had natural talent, it takes a lot more than that to become a rugby legend. He was also mentally strong, super-competitive, and always worked hard to stay at the top of his game. He used to practise with a ball filled with sand to increase the distance of his passing, and to improve his accuracy, he would often attempt to throw it through a swinging tyre!

Gareth was fortunate to play during a golden age of Welsh rugby, but even alongside fly-half Barry John and so many other top teammates, he was still able to stand out, which is a sign of true greatness. And so is being knighted by Queen Elizabeth II for services to sport, which happened to Sir Gareth in 2015.

Sadly, I didn't get to see Gareth play live, but I feel like I have because I've seen the video of "that try" so many times! It's one of the most inspiring rugby moments, ever!

GEORGE GREGAN

SCRUM-HALF

POSITION **SCRUM-HALF**

DATE OF BIRTH **19 APRIL 1973**

COUNTRY **AUSTRALIA**

CLUBS **BRUMBIES, TOULON, SUNTORY SUNGOLIATH**

SUPERSTAR MOMENT **WINNING THE 1999 MEN'S RUGBY WORLD CUP WITH AUSTRALIA**

FUN FACT **HIS MIDDLE NAME, "MUSARURWA" MEANS "CHOSEN ONE" IN SHONA, ONE OF THE OFFICIAL LANGUAGES OF ZIMBABWE, WHERE HIS MOTHER WAS FROM.**

GEORGE GREGAN

Gareth Edwards might be one of the game's greatest all-round scrum-halves, but the greatest passer? Well, no one has ever moved the ball better than George Gregan.

George was born in Zambia, in South-Central Africa, but when he was just two, his family moved to Australia, where his father was from. There he started playing rugby league, but at secondary school George switched to rugby union, and quickly found a position that suited him perfectly. He was small, agile, loved to talk and be at the centre of the action ... oh, and he could pass the ball really well. Yes, that's right – he was a superstar scrum-half in the making!

George was only 21 when he made his senior debut for Australia, but was he really big and brave enough to play international rugby? George soon showed just how strong he was in the 1994 Bledisloe Cup against Australia's biggest rivals, New Zealand.

With the All Blacks trailing by a single point, their winger Jeff Wilson stormed past one tackle and then another, until he was racing towards the try line. Surely he would score? But no, out of nowhere, across came Australia's new number 9 with a fantastic flying tackle! The Wallabies went on to win the game, and George went on to be their starting scrum-half for the next twelve years.

His first World Cup in 1995 ended in a quarter-final defeat to England, but at the tournament four years later, it felt like a completely different Australia team. For the 1999 Men's Rugby World Cup, George was still there at scrum-half, but he had a new number 10 by his side, Stephen Larkham. They had already formed a successful partnership for their club, Brumbies, and now they were about to do the same for their country.

In the quarter-finals against Wales, George was the hero with two tries.

In the semi-finals against South Africa, it was Larkham's turn, winning the game with a drop goal in extra time.

And in the final against France? Well, that was a real team effort, but George provided the moment of the match with "that pass". Collecting the ball from the lineout, he faked to throw it one way, but instead, played a beautiful behind-the-back flick pass the other way to flanker Owen

Finegan, who ran all the way through to score and seal the victory for Australia.

In 2001, George became the new Australia captain, but could he lead the Wallabies to World Cup glory again in 2003? As always, he gave it everything, even scoring a drop goal against Ireland! This time, however, his Australia team were defeated in the final by England.

When he finally retired in 2007, after a fourth World Cup, George had played 139 matches for his country, 59 of those as captain. He waved goodbye to the game as a World Champion, a record-breaking rugby legend and the ultimate pass-master.

MAGGIE'S INSIGHTS

George changed the way players approached the game, by showing that being a good rugby player isn't all about what you can do on the field; it is also about what you know and how you use that knowledge. I now work with him as a pundit and he's always willing to share insights to help the people around him.

★ RISING STAR ★

CAM ROIGARD
SCRUM-HALF

POSITION **SCRUM-HALF**

DATE OF BIRTH **16 NOVEMBER 2000**

COUNTRY **NEW ZEALAND**

CLUBS **COUNTIES MANUKAU, HURRICANES**

SUPERSTAR MOMENT **SCORING A BRILLIANT SOLO TRY AGAINST SOUTH AFRICA IN 2023**

FUN FACT **AS A KID, CAM WAS ALSO A VERY SUCCESSFUL SPEEDWAY RACING DRIVER. HE FINISHED SECOND AT THE NEW ZEALAND CHAMPIONSHIPS IN 2019.**

CAM ROIGARD

New Zealand's Cam Roigard is not your typical scrum-half. For a start, he's 1.83 metres (6 ft) tall and weighs nearly 90 kg, but that was never going to stop him from playing his favourite position.

"I was small when I was younger," he says, "but then from about sixteen to nineteen, I had a growth spurt. I probably wasn't the ideal build for a scrum-half at that point, but I never thought of moving… I played a different game."

What Cam lacks in agility and a low centre of gravity, he more than makes up for with his power on the attack. Plus, he can really zip a quick pass for a big guy!

After his growth spurt, Cam decided to model his game on New Zealand international TJ Perenara, another tall scrum-half who is also left-handed and -footed. Fast-forward a few years to 2021, and Cam signed for the Hurricanes … the same club as his hero!

His first year with the Hurricanes was a great opportunity to watch TJ up close and pick up lots of tips. But when Perenara injured himself badly in 2022, suddenly Cam had the chance to start at scrum-half for the Hurricanes. In a breakout performance against the Waratahs, he scored two tries that brilliantly showed off his strength and skill.

A new star was born! As the tries kept coming, Cam was called up to the New Zealand squad for the 2023 Rugby Championship, and on his debut against Australia, he played a part in setting up two late tries.

A month later, New Zealand suffered a heavy defeat against South Africa in a warm-up match ahead of the 2023 Men's Rugby World Cup. But the one bright spark? A sensational solo try from their super-sub scrum-half! Cam grabbed a loose ball, spotted a gap in the Springbok defence, and – *ZOOM!* – he was off, racing 70 yards, and past two tackles, to score for the first time in international rugby.

At the World Cup, Cam was picked to start in New Zealand's second match, against Namibia, and he made an instant impact again, scoring two tries within seven minutes! The first was good, but the second was sublime, finished with a dummy pass and then a spin over the line. Woah, the kid had serious skills, and he continued to shine with a breakaway assist against Italy, and then another try against Uruguay, featuring another outrageous dummy.

After his electric start to the World Cup, Cam unfortunately didn't get any game-time in the knock-out rounds as New Zealand picked Aaron Smith and Finlay Christie instead. But with Smith retiring after the tournament, the scrum-half role is now up for grabs. Unfortunately, a bad knee injury kept Cam out of the 2024 Rugby Championship, but he made a triumphant return to the New Zealand team in November with back-to-back tries against France and Italy, and he's now looking better than ever.

> At the 2023 Men's Rugby World Cup, Cam emerged as a really exciting talent. He is quick and is always a threat when he has his hands on the ball. I expect him to have a bright future with the All Blacks, if he can stay fit and injury-free.

★ MODERN HERO ★

FAF DE KLERK
SCRUM-HALF

POSITION **SCRUM-HALF**

DATE OF BIRTH **19 OCTOBER 1991**

COUNTRY **SOUTH AFRICA**

CLUBS **LIONS, SALE SHARKS, YOKOHAMA CANON EAGLES**

SUPERSTAR MOMENT **WINNING THE 2019 AND 2023 MEN'S RUGBY WORLD CUPS WITH SOUTH AFRICA**

FUN FACT **WHEN HE WON THE WORLD CUP IN 2019, FAF WAS SEEN CELEBRATING WEARING ONLY A PAIR OF PANTS WITH THE SOUTH AFRICA FLAG ON THEM!**

FAF DE KLERK

On the rugby pitch, François "Faf" de Klerk is a nightmare to play against: aggressive, annoying, energetic and loud. But if he's on your team? Well, then he's an absolute hero!

These days, Faf's a two-time World Champion, but as a young player, his small size was a big problem. Eventually, however, after lots of hard work and disappointment, he made his professional rugby dream come true, signing for Johannesburg's Lions in 2014. Then, two years of impressive performances later, he was called up to make his international debut for South Africa.

Hurray, a happy ending! Not so fast. In 2016, the South Africa rugby team lost eight of their eleven games, and Faf was part of every painful defeat, including one against Wales where he was shown a yellow card. It was a disastrous start, and, surprise, surprise – Faf was soon dropped from the team.

What now? Well, instead of staying in South Africa, Faf made a big and very brave move to England, to sign for Sale Sharks. He wouldn't be able to represent his country while playing for a foreign club, but Faf was looking ahead to the future. If he could become a superstar at Sale, then he might still make it back into the Springbok team in time to play at the 2019 Men's Rugby World Cup.

And that's exactly what he did. At Sale, Faf took his scrum-half skills to a new level, and he was at the centre of everything, even kicking conversions and penalties, like he used to when he played fly-half at school.

Faf finished the 2017–18 season on the shortlist for the Premiership Player of the Season award, and, with South Africa changing their rules, he also became a Springbok again. Faf had earned a second chance, and this time, he was better, stronger, and more determined than ever to make that number 9 shirt his own.

Mission accomplished! At the 2019 Men's Rugby World Cup, Faf was South Africa's first-choice scrum-half and, like the team around him, he got better and better as the tournament went on. In the quarter-finals against Japan, Faf scored a rare try, but his main role was to fight for every ball and guide his team to victory, which he did brilliantly in the semi-finals against Wales and then the final against England. Wow, they had done it; South Africa had bounced back to win the World Cup!

Four years later, Faf was back again for the 2023 Men's Rugby World Cup, but this time, he had to share the number 9 shirt with Cobus Reinach. No problem! "My role was to try and inject a bit of energy and body language into the team," Faf said after a super-sub performance in the semi-final against England.

So, which scrum-half would start in the final against New Zealand? In the end, South Africa chose Faf for his experience, his energy, and his endless fighting spirit. And the result? The Springboks won the World Cup again!

The message of this story? As Faf says, "What matters is the size of your heart rather than your body. If you are ready to work hard you will reach your dreams."

Faf has been there and done it all. Even though he is a double World Champion with plenty of young players snapping at his heels, he still looks hungry and busy. He remains a hero to many.

★ MODERN HERO ★

ANTOINE DUPONT
SCRUM-HALF

POSITION **SCRUM-HALF**

DATE OF BIRTH **15 NOVEMBER 1996**

COUNTRY **FRANCE**

CLUBS **CASTRES, TOULOUSE**

SUPERSTAR MOMENT **WHERE DO WE START? THERE ARE SO MANY!**

FUN FACT **ANTOINE HAS BRAINS AS WELL AS BALL SKILLS. IN 2021, HE COMPLETED A MASTER'S DEGREE IN SPORT MANAGEMENT.**

ANTOINE DUPONT

Three Six Nations Men's Player of the Championship awards, two European Rugby Champions Cups, two Six Nations titles, one World Rugby Men's Player of the Year award, and one Gold Medal in the Men's Rugby Sevens at the 2024 Olympic Games – Antoine Dupont has already achieved so much and he's still in his prime!

Antoine started playing rugby aged four at his local club, Magnoac FC, in South-West France, before joining professional club Auch, aged fifteen. There, he trained and played alongside future France teammate Grégory Alldritt, but it was at the 2016 World Rugby Under-20 Championship in England that Antoine really broke through, scoring five tries, even though France finished way down in ninth place.

Woah, future superstar alert! A year later, Antoine was making his debut for the France senior team in the 2016 Six Nations. It would be another few years before Antoine became his country's starting scrum-half, but once that number 9 shirt was his, he changed the game completely.

In terms of his size, Antoine is a typical scrum-half – 1.75 metres (5 ft 9 in), 85 kg – which gives him a low centre of gravity and great balance. But what makes him so special is all the other stuff on top: the pace, the power (in attack and defence), the vision to spot the smallest gaps in any defence, and the skill to deliver the perfect pass or to beat any opponent.

Oh, and he's also an awesome leader. In France, they call the scrum-half "le petit général" ("the little general"), and that's exactly what Antoine is – he runs the game and makes everything tick for his team.

When France won a Six Nations Grand Slam in 2022, Antoine was sensational, starring in every match and in every area of the game. In the crucial final game against England, he even raced through to score his side's final try.

The 2023 Men's Rugby World Cup in France was all set to be Antoine's defining moment but, unfortunately, he fractured his cheekbone in their second game against Namibia. Antoine bravely made it back for the quarter-final against South Africa, but unfortunately he couldn't save his country from a 29–28 defeat.

Oooof, so close – that's gotta hurt, right? But that's another thing about Antoine: he's really resilient. He bounced straight back to lead

Toulouse to a second Champions Cup, and in the final, Antoine was absolutely phenomenal, beating the most defenders, winning the most turnovers, AND making the most tackles, while also doing all the usual scrum-half stuff like passing and kicking.

And next, to the 2024 Paris Olympics. In front of a home crowd, could Antoine inspire France to glory in the rugby sevens? Of course he could – even though it's not his natural game, everything he touches turns to gold! In the final against Fiji, Antoine came off the bench to set up a sensational try and then score two more of his own.

After that Gold Medal moment, Antoine returned to rugby union and led France to the 2025 Six Nations title, despite missing the last match through injury.

No wonder his teammates call him the Martian – because Antoine is simply out of this world!

MAGGIE'S INSIGHTS

He's the best number 9 in the world. I have always been in awe of Antoine, not only based on what he does on the field, but also how he is able to manage the pressure, the weight of expectations put on him by his nation. He leads from the front and is an example for all.

★ GAMECHANGER ★

LAURE SANSUS
SCRUM-HALF

POSITION **SCRUM-HALF**

DATE OF BIRTH **21 JUNE 1994**

COUNTRY **FRANCE**

CLUBS **TOULOUSE**

SUPERSTAR MOMENT **WINNING PLAYER OF THE TOURNAMENT AT THE 2022 WOMEN'S SIX NATIONS**

FUN FACT **HAVING PLAYED ALONGSIDE HER WIFE, PAULINE BOURDON, FOR MANY YEARS, LAURE NOW COACHES HER AT TOULOUSE!**

LAURE SANSUS (NOW BOURDON-SANSUS)

2022 was a great year for French scrum-halves! In the Men's Six Nations, Antoine Dupont led France to a Grand Slam, and in the women's tournament, it was Laure Sansus' time to shine.

Laure, or Loulou as her teammates call her, had been playing rugby since she was just four years old and for France since 2016, but at last, in 2022, her breakthrough moment arrived. Why had it taken her so long?

Well, at 1.57 metres (5 ft 2 in) tall, Laure was always destined to be a scrum-half, but unfortunately for her, she wasn't the only talented young player fighting for the France number 9 shirt. The name of her rival? Pauline Bourdon, who years later, would become Laure's wife…

But first, back to 2016. That year, Laure was the back-up scrum-half as France won the Women's Six Nations, but because of injuries and personal issues, she had to wait until 2020 to make her next Women's Six Nations appearance. And in her comeback match against England? Laure plucked the ball out of a ruck, played a cheeky one-two, and threw herself over the try line!

Laure scored three more thrilling tries against Italy and Wales, but the tournament was suspended partway through because of the Covid-19 pandemic, and at the next tournament in 2021, Laure and Pauline took turns at number 9, with neither able to truly shine.

So, what was the answer? In early 2022, Pauline picked up an injury, which meant Laure had the whole 2022 Six Nations to star for France. In a world of scrum-halves who preferred to pass rather than run, Laure was about to get the ball and *gooooo...*

Against Ireland, she was incredible: throwing dummies, finding gaps, and scoring two tries. Against Scotland, she was sensational: kicking, chasing, and scoring twice. And against Wales, she was wonderful: spinning her way out of tackles, and scoring another two tries.

Six in three games ... from a scrum-half? Wow, what a gamechanger! Although France lost the title decider to England, Laure finished with the most tries, the most try-assists, and ... the Player of the Tournament award!

Laure refused to take all the glory for herself, though. "When you're in my position, the forwards play a massive part in your success," she said. "To be noticed as a scrum-half, I really owe it to the whole team."

Sadly, Laure's superstar moment didn't last long, though. She announced that she would be retiring after the Women's Rugby World Cup in 2022, aged 28, to focus on other things, like starting a family with Pauline. *Noooooooo!* It was sad news, but could she say goodbye in style at the World Cup?

Laure scored two tries in the opening match against South Africa, but in France's next game against England, she was stretchered off with a serious knee injury, and that was it: the end of Laure's brief but brilliant rugby career. They say it only takes one moment to change a game; or in this case, one Six Nations.

MAGGIE'S INSIGHTS

Laure really shook up women's rugby. When I saw her play in the 2022 Women's Six Nations, she stood out for being a pocket rocket, finding gaps in the defence where there were none. She could change a game in the blink of an eye, and she also changed the way the game was played.

★ GAMECHANGER ★

AGUSTÍN PICHOT
SCRUM-HALF

POSITION **SCRUM-HALF**

DATE OF BIRTH **22 AUGUST 1974**

COUNTRY **ARGENTINA**

CLUBS **CLUB ATLÉTICO DE SAN ISIDRO, RICHMOND, BRISTOL, STADE FRANÇAIS, RACING MÉTRO**

SUPERSTAR MOMENT **LEADING ARGENTINA TO A THIRD-PLACE FINISH AT THE 2007 MEN'S RUGBY WORLD CUP**

FUN FACT **IN 2016, AGUSTÍN WAS VOTED THE SPORT'S MOST INFLUENTIAL FIGURE BY *RUGBY WORLD* MAGAZINE.**

AGUSTÍN PICHOT

For many years, international rugby was ruled by The Big Five: England, France, Australia, New Zealand, and South Africa. Doesn't sound very fair, does it? As both a player and now as an official, Agustín Pichot has fought harder than anyone to change the game and make rugby a sport for all.

Agustín played his first match for his country in 1995, the year that most of the rugby world went from amateur (unpaid) to professional (paid). Argentina, however, decided to stay amateur, which meant that although their national team, the Pumas, had been part of the Men's Rugby World Cup since 1987, their players still had no proper training facilities, and earned no money from the game.

Over the next 20 years, Agustín would help change all that. Off the pitch, he worked hard to win rights for the players and turn the old-school Argentine Rugby Union into a proper, professional organization. And on the pitch, Agustín set high standards and pushed the players around him to keep improving, and dreaming big. Why couldn't "little" Argentina win the Rugby World Cup? Anything was possible!

In 1997, Agustín moved to England and continued to play club rugby in Europe for over twenty years. But for all his success there, Agustín's number-one focus was always Argentina. How could he help them compete at the highest level?

In 2000, Agustín became the new national team captain, and one by one, year by year, he led the Pumas to victories over each of the Six Nations teams, ending with England in 2006. That was real progress, but Agustín always wanted more for his country. Their next aim was to shine at the Men's Rugby World Cup.

After reaching the quarter-finals in 1999, Argentina had been knocked out early in 2003, but could they do better in 2007? "This team has a hunger to write history," their inspirational leader said after they beat France in their opening game.

As a feisty scrum-half, Agustín was the heartbeat of the Argentina team. With his socks always rolled down around his ankles, he didn't stop moving – chasing down opponents, making clever runs – and the Pumas couldn't stop winning: against Georgia, Namibia, Ireland, and then against Scotland in the quarter-finals. Hurray, they had made history – Argentina were into the World Cup semi-finals for the first time ever! There, they lost to South Africa, but they bounced back to claim third place. What an achievement for "little" Argentina!

After retiring from the national team in 2008, Agustín then led a campaign for Argentina to join the Rugby Championship – alongside Australia, New Zealand, and South Africa – which finally happened in 2012. When the Pumas won their first match in the competition, against Australia in 2014, their centre Juan Martín Hernández dedicated the victory to Agustín, the hero who had done so much to make his country's rugby team great, and to change the game for the better.

Agustín has influenced me on my journey to try to bring about change too, in a sport that at times can be resistant to it. He taught me to not be afraid to champion what I believe in, even though my views may not please everyone.

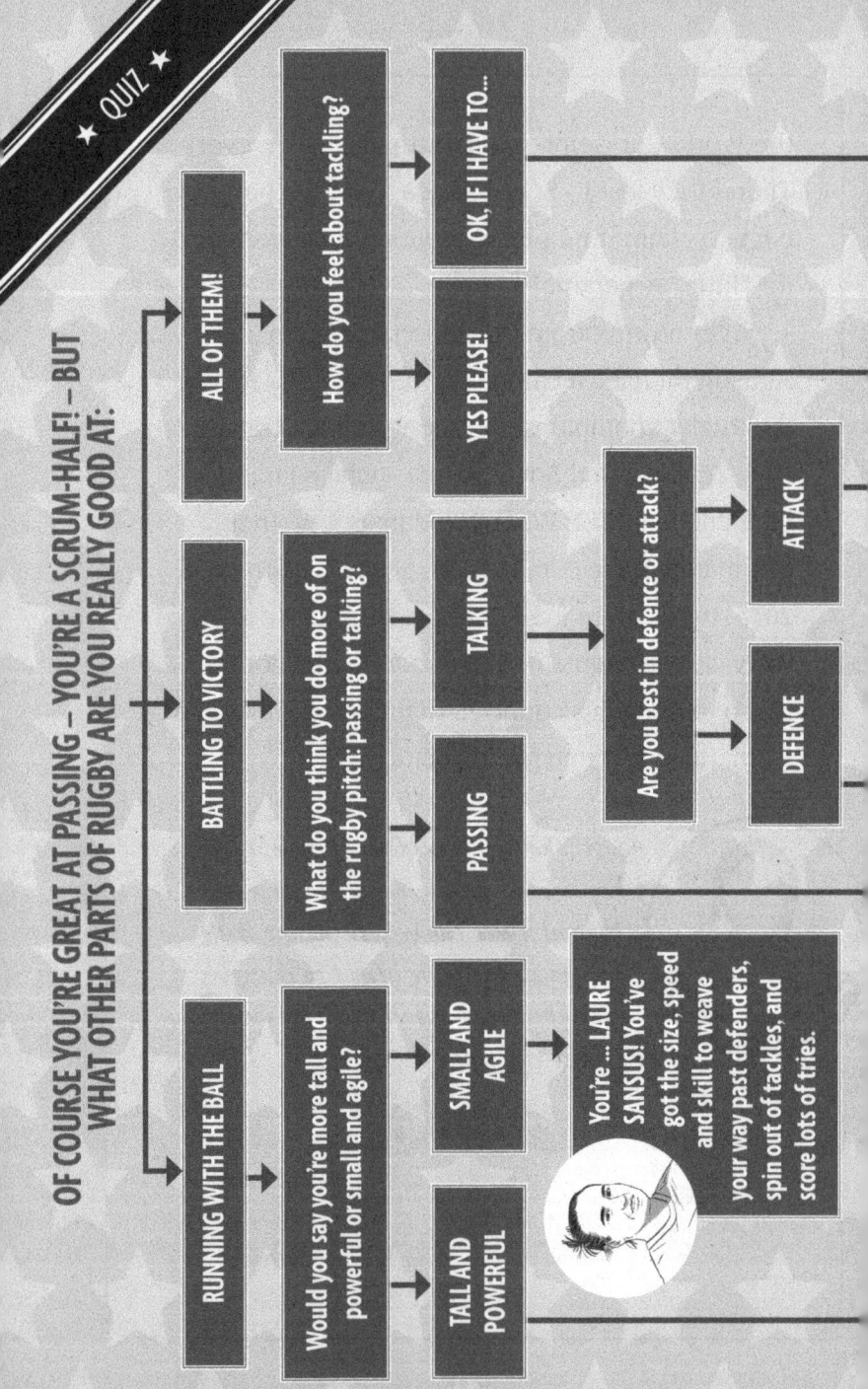

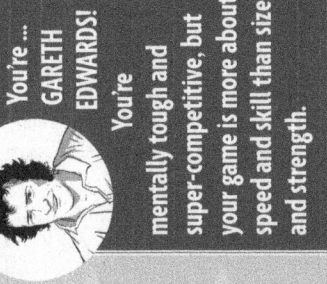

You're ... GARETH EDWARDS! You're mentally tough and super-competitive, but your game is more about speed and skill than size and strength.

You're ... ANTOINE DUPONT! You're the scrum-half superstar who really has got it all: pace, power (in attack and defence), vision and skill.

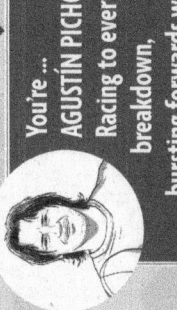

You're ... AGUSTÍN PICHOT! Racing to every breakdown, bursting forwards with the ball – you never stop moving and you never stop fighting for your team.

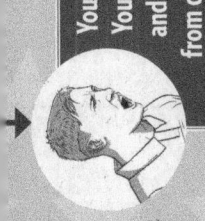

You're ... CAM ROIGARD! You've got the size, speed and skill to break away from defenders, burst through tackles, and score lots of tries.

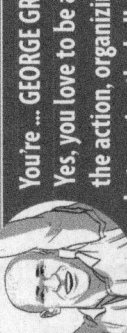

You're ... GEORGE GREGAN! Yes, you love to be at the centre of the action, organizing everything, but moving the ball quickly and accurately is what you do most, and best.

You're ... FAF DE KLERK! Your opponents might find you aggressive, annoying, and a nightmare to play against, but your teammates think you're an absolute hero!

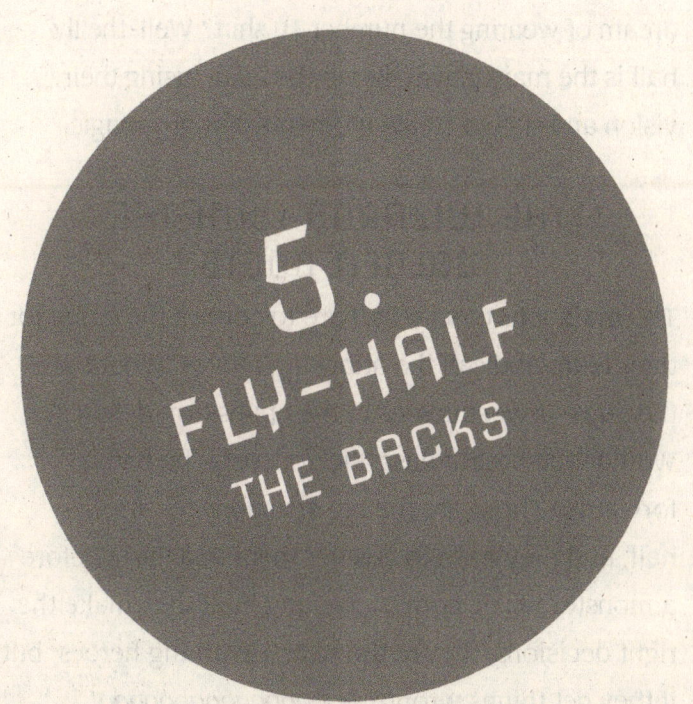

5.
FLY-HALF
THE BACKS

From scrum-half, we're passing on to one of rugby's most popular positions ... the fly-half. The name of this position is short for "flying half-back" and has nothing to do with insects. Why do so many people dream of wearing the number 10 shirt? Well, the fly-half is the main playmaker in the team, using their vision and skill to create moments of rugby magic.

THE WIZARDS WITH THE GOLDEN BOOTS

The main jobs of a fly-half are to control the game for their team and call the attacking moves. Where are the gaps or weaknesses in the opposition defence? Would it be best to pass, kick or carry the ball forwards? Those are the big questions for any fly-half, and they have to answer them in a flash, before a monster tackle comes crashing in. If they make the right decisions, they're the match-winning heroes, but if they get things wrong? *Boooooooooooooooo!*

This is rugby we're talking about, so no player gets away with doing zero dirty work, but the number 10s do often get to keep their faces the cleanest, while also getting lots of the glory and praise for setting up tries, and often kicking **conversions**, **penalties** and **drop goals**.

RUGBY RULES

KICKING POINTS

There are three ways you can score points through kicking. The ball always has to be kicked over the bar of the goalposts

1. A **CONVERSION**: a kick to add an extra two points after a try is scored. It is taken from a point in line with where the ball was touched down. The kicker can decide exactly how far away.

2. A **PENALTY**: a kick to score three points after the opposition has given away a foul. It is taken from the place where the foul is committed.

For conversions and penalties, the play stops and the ball is kicked off a tee on the grass. But that's not the case when it comes to...

3. A **DROP GOAL**: a player can attempt a drop goal at any moment in open play, but they're really difficult because the game is still being played and you can't just boot the ball out of your hand. Instead, the ball has to touch the ground before it's kicked high between the posts. It's a tricky technique and guess which player tends to be the best at scoring drop goals... Yep, the fly-half!

TO BE A FLY-HALF SUPERSTAR YOU NEED:

1. Skilful hands and feet

A fly-half needs to have the full set of rugby skills: running, tackling, catching, but especially passing and kicking. The best fly-halves can pass perfectly off both hands and do it accurately every time, even under extreme pressure. They're also brilliant at kicking the ball with either their left or right foot – both out of their hands and off a tee.

2. Killer creativity

The fly-half needs great vision to see what is happening in front of them and then use that information to decide what to do next. The best fly-halves can see what will happen two or three phases ahead. Good vision helps a number 10 to understand where best to position their players or place the ball.

3. Strong leadership skills

A superstar number 10 needs to be a top decision-maker. They don't have much time to call the moves, so they need to think and act fast, while keeping calm and composed. They must also be able to communicate the decisions clearly, so that everyone around them understands what they have to do next.

KICKING KINGS AND QUEENS

Any rugby player in any position can take the kicks for their team, but it's most likely to be the fly-half.

STATS

- Legendary New Zealand number 10 **Dan Carter** (2003–15) holds the men's world records for: most international points (1,598), most conversions (293) and most penalties (281) scored.
- England fly-half **Jonny Wilkinson** (1998–2011), meanwhile, has the most World Cup points (277), and the most drop goals scored (36) in the men's game.

- **Simon Culhane** scored a record-setting 45 points in a single match at the 1995 Men's Rugby World Cup, as New Zealand thrashed Japan 145–17. And the best part? Culhane only scored one try, with the rest of his points coming from twenty conversions!
- France's number 10 **Caroline Drouin** had a wonderful 2021 Women's Rugby World Cup, scoring twelve out of fourteen conversions, plus four out of five penalties.
- In the 2024 Women's Six Nations, Ireland's young fly-half **Dannah O'Brien** was on fire, kicking ten successful conversions out of twelve.

THE FLY-HALF THEN ...

In the old days, fly-halves were encouraged to just let their creativity flow. For legendary Welsh wizard Barry John (1966–72), the plan was very simple: "You throw it, I will catch it," he famously told his scrum-half Gareth Edwards, and the rest is rugby history!

... V. THE FLY-HALF NOW

These days, fly-halves can still be clever and creative, but they also have to be really organized and tactical, often acting like another team coach on the pitch.

SO, WHICH KIND OF FLY-HALF WOULD YOU BE?

Will you be a kicking king or queen, or a passing prince or princess? Will you be the playmaker, setting up lots of tries for your teammates, or will you have the speed and skill to race through and score yourself?

To help you decide, here's a look at some of the best fly-halves rugby has ever seen, all with different styles and approaches. Then take our quiz to find out which superstar you would be.

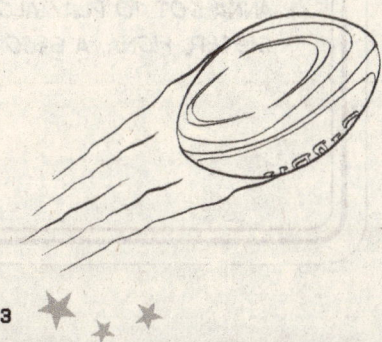

ANNA RICHARDS

FLY-HALF

POSITION **FLY-HALF**

DATE OF BIRTH **3 DECEMBER 1964**

COUNTRY **NEW ZEALAND**

CLUBS **AUCKLAND**

SUPERSTAR MOMENTS **ALL FOUR OF HER WORLD CUP WINS!**

FUN FACT **AT THE 1998 WOMEN'S RUGBY WORLD CUP, ANNA GOT TO PLAY ALONGSIDE HER YOUNGER SISTER, FIONA, A SECOND ROWER.**

ANNA RICHARDS

Rugby legends don't get any greater than Anna Richards. During her incredible, twenty-year international career, she won the Women's Rugby World Cup a record four times, and who knows, maybe it might have been five if New Zealand hadn't missed the tournament in 1994!

For such a successful rugby player, Anna came to the game very late. As a kid growing up in Timaru, a small city on New Zealand's South Island, she played lots of tennis and netball, but at that time, rugby wasn't really an option for girls and there was no national team.

"I'd always watched rugby," Anna said, "getting up in the early hours of the morning to watch the All Blacks play, but I never actually thought I'd play rugby."

When she was dropped from the University of Canterbury netball team, aged 21, Anna was invited to train with the women's rugby team instead, and once she started playing, she never wanted to stop! Soon, she was setting off on an amazing seven-week tour, playing matches across America and Europe.

In 1990, the Black Ferns, the New Zealand women's rugby team, was formed, and a year later, an unofficial Women's Rugby World Cup was organized in Wales. Anna couldn't wait; she was one of 26 players who made the long trip, despite having to pay for their own travel.

The Black Ferns lost to the USA in the semi-finals, but that defeat only spurred Anna on even more. Back home in New Zealand, she carried on starring for her club, Auckland, while also working part-time as a lawyer. Then, when the first official Women's Rugby World Cup took place in Amsterdam in 1998, Anna was ready to shine, and so were her talented teammates. This time, the Black Ferns went all the way to win the World Cup, and they did it again in 2002 ... and in 2006, too!

By 2010, Anna was 45 years old and ready to retire, but when the Black Ferns called on her to be a last-minute replacement in the 2010 Women's Rugby World Cup, she couldn't say no. She didn't just sit on the subs bench, though; no, she played a starring role, scoring a try in the semi-final against France, and then using all her experience, calm and intelligence to help her team beat

England in the final. Wow, she had won her fourth World Cup in her last-ever match!

So, that's the story of Anna Richards, the super-successful superstar who paved the way in women's rugby. But what was she like as a fly-half? Well, she didn't really kick conversions or penalties for New Zealand, and she didn't score many tries either. No, her main role was to be the playmaker, controlling the game and creating chance after chance for her teammates. And when it comes to vision and passing, Anna is still the GOAT in the women's game.

MAGGIE'S INSIGHTS

I had the pleasure (and pain!) of playing against Anna in the 2010 Women's Rugby World Cup final. As a number 7 my role was to target the fly-half, but in that match she was invincible. Even though I was 26 and she was 45, she still got up after every tackle I made on her, as she led the Black Ferns to another World Cup title.

LEGEND

DAN CARTER
FLY-HALF

POSITION **FLY-HALF**

DATE OF BIRTH **5 MARCH 1982**

COUNTRY **NEW ZEALAND**

CLUBS **CANTERBURY, CRUSADERS, PERPIGNAN, RACING 92, KOBELCO STEELERS**

SUPERSTAR MOMENT **HIS PLAYER-OF-THE-MATCH PERFORMANCE IN THE 2015 MEN'S RUGBY WORLD CUP FINAL**

FUN FACT **HE ONCE MET THE OWNER OF NFL SIDE THE NEW ENGLAND PATRIOTS ABOUT POTENTIALLY JOINING THE TEAM AS A KICKER!**

DAN CARTER

From one legendary New Zealand fly-half to another. While Dan Carter will be best remembered for his brilliantly accurate left boot, it was his all-round game that made him such a world-class, World Cup-winning talent.

As journalist Andy Bull puts it, "Carter passed like a scrum-half, hit like a flanker; sprinted, stepped and finished like a winger in attack; caught, kicked and tackled like a full-back in defence... The great fly-halves are all good in different ways; Carter was good in every way."

Yes, Dan had the size and skill to play any position, really, but he was definitely at his best as a number 10. Playing for New Zealand in rugby's most popular position, however, is one of the game's greatest challenges. When Dan made his international debut in 2003, at the age of 21, Carlos Spencer was the first-choice fly-half, but Dan was determined to make the role his own. A year later, he succeeded, and the rest is rugby history.

In 2005, Dan led New Zealand to victory against the British and Irish Lions, scoring 33 points in the second Test, including two terrific tries, which earned him the first of his THREE World Rugby Men's Player of the Year awards!

Between 2005 and 2008, New Zealand won four Tri Nations series (this later became the Rugby Championships when Argentina joined in 2012) in a row against Australia and South Africa, and guess who was their top scorer! Yes, Dan the man! In 2010, he scored a penalty from the halfway line against Wales to become the highest points scorer in the history of men's international rugby. Wow, and he was still only 28!

At that stage, there was only one thing missing for Dan: a World Cup trophy. In 2003, he watched from the subs bench as Australia shocked New Zealand by defeating them in the semi-finals. In 2007, he limped off with a calf injury as New Zealand lost to France in the quarter-finals. Four years later, the All Blacks bounced back to win the 2011 Men's Rugby World Cup, but they had to do it without their phenomenal fly-half. Again, he picked up an injury, this time in the group stage.

Poor Dan! The 2015 tournament would be his last chance to star in international rugby. Could he stay fit and shine bright? Oh yes, he could! In the semi-finals, New Zealand were losing to South

Africa, until Dan stepped up with a sensational drop goal, followed by an assist for Beauden Barrett's winning try. Then in the final against Australia, Dan kept calm and fired his team to glory, scoring four high-pressure penalties, as well as an even better drop goal. And to finish? One last conversion, this time with his weaker right foot!

"Basically, it was a tribute to my father," Dan explained later. All the hours they had spent together in the garden practising kicks with both feet had paid off on the biggest stage of all.

MAGGIE'S INSIGHTS

What more can I say about Dan? He's a true rugby legend! He left a mark on the game and his composure and drive for excellence was remarkable. He knew how to handle pressure and always seemed in control. When he played, he looked like he had all the time in the world to make a decision. His composure was infectious and that brought the best out of the players around him. He often would carry the weight of the nation (and the jersey!) on his shoulders but never let it show. He was one unique player.

★ RISING STAR ★

PAOLO GARBISI
FLY-HALF

POSITION **FLY-HALF**

DATE OF BIRTH **26 APRIL 2000**

COUNTRY **ITALY**

CLUBS **MOGLIANO, PETRARCA, BENETTON, MONTPELLIER, TOULON**

SUPERSTAR MOMENT **KICKING THE CONVERSION TO CLINCH ITALY'S FIRST SIX NATIONS WIN IN SEVEN YEARS, AGAINST WALES IN 2022**

FUN FACT **PAOLO'S OTHER PASSION IS FASHION. HIS GRANDFATHER FOUNDED A CLOTHING COMPANY IN VENICE, WHICH HIS MOTHER STILL WORKS FOR.**

PAOLO GARBISI

When Italy joined England, Wales, Scotland, Ireland and France to form the "Six Nations" tournament back in 2000, their players and fans were so excited. Sure, the Azzurri (the Blues) had some catching up to do with Europe's biggest countries, but the future looked bright as they won their first-ever Six Nations match against Scotland.

After that excellent start, however, Italy lost every match in 2001 and 2002, and soon the rugby world was wondering if they had made a big mistake by letting them join. By 2020, those doubts were getting louder because the Azzurri hadn't won a single game since 2015!

But luckily there was light at the end of the losing tunnel for Italy. A new generation of exciting and talented young players was about to emerge, led by winger Ange Capuozzo and fly-half Paolo Garbisi. Hurray, at last!

Ever since legendary player Diego Dominguez's retirement in 2003, Italy had been searching for a top new number 10, and now they had finally found one! Paolo is tall and strong for a fly-half, but he prefers to use his power to burst past opponents on the attack. "I have to be honest with you," he says, "I don't like defending." He began playing rugby aged six for his local club, Mogliano, and took up kicking a few years later, after being inspired by watching New Zealand's Dan Carter, who was left-footed just like him.

"I was not really thinking about rugby as a career when I was younger," Paolo admits. "I wanted to be a lawyer. It was only once I was in the Italy Under-20 team that I thought something might happen."

And it did! In October 2020, Paolo was selected to make his senior debut for Italy in the Six Nations against Ireland. Although his team lost, he kicked both conversions, plus one penalty, and then finished it off with a sensational solo try!

It was a very promising start for Paolo, but what he wanted most was to help his team to win. Unfortunately, that first victory didn't come in 2020, or 2021. But in 2022, against Wales, the Azzurri scored a try with seconds to go. Now, if they could just score the conversion, Italy would win…

This was it; the massive moment Paolo had been waiting for. BOOM! – he calmly fired the ball straight between the posts and then collapsed to the grass, crying tears of pure joy. They had done it; Italy had ended their 36-game Six Nations losing streak at last!

And an exciting new era had just begun. In November 2022, Italy beat Australia for the first time ever, and in the 2024 Six Nations, they came very close to beating England, and even closer to beating France. With the scores tied at 13–13, Paolo had a last-minute chance to win it, but when the ball rolled off the tee, he had to rush his kick and it struck the post.

Nooooooo! So close! Would that miss knock Paolo's confidence? No way! He bounced back to kick and push his team to victories over Scotland and Wales. Now, that's the sign of a true rugby superstar.

Paolo is resilient and not afraid to step up to the mark when asked. He is a star in the making and is already showing a level of maturity beyond his years.

★ MODERN HERO ★

MARCUS SMITH
FLY-HALF

POSITION **FLY-HALF, FULL-BACK**

DATE OF BIRTH **14 FEBRUARY 1999**

COUNTRY **ENGLAND**

CLUBS **HARLEQUINS**

SUPERSTAR MOMENT **SCORING A LAST-MINUTE DROP GOAL AS ENGLAND BEAT IRELAND IN THE 2024 SIX NATIONS**

FUN FACT **HIS FAVOURITE SUBJECT AT SCHOOL? "I LOVE MATHS, BECAUSE I LIKE A CHALLENGE."**

MARCUS SMITH

For years, Marcus Smith was seen as the "Golden Boy" of England rugby, but now, he's an experienced star and a modern hero.

Marcus was born in the Philippines, but aged seven he moved with his family to Singapore, and that's where his rugby journey began. Inspired by his dad, Jeremy (who played for Hong Kong in the 1990s), and watching the famous Hong Kong Rugby Sevens tournament, Marcus joined his local club, Centaurs RFC.

Alongside rugby, however, Marcus also loved playing football. So, which sport would he choose to focus on?

"When I first came back to England aged thirteen, I preferred football," he admits. But two things changed his mind: 1. he won a sports scholarship to Brighton College, where rugby was the main sport, and 2. he was rejected by the Tottenham Hotspur football academy.

Right, rugby it was, then! At Brighton College, Marcus switched from scrum-half to fly-half and quickly became his school's star player. By eighteen, he was making his professional debut for

Harlequins at Twickenham, and training with the England senior team, alongside two of his fly-half heroes, Owen Farrell and George Ford!

For the next few years, Marcus spent lots of time with the England team – watching, learning, even practising his kicking with 2003 Men's Rugby World Cup hero Jonny Wilkinson – but when would he get the chance to actually play? In 2021, Marcus finally made his full England debut in a win against the USA, scoring four conversions, plus a first try! A few months later, he followed that up with a last-minute penalty to beat South Africa.

Then in the 2022 Men's Six Nations, England's "Golden Boy" finally hit the big time! With Farrell and Ford both out, Marcus took his chance brilliantly, winning two Player of the Match awards and finishing as the Championship's top scorer. Surely, his time had come?

But no, at the 2023 Six Nations, Marcus was back on the bench. At 1.75 metres (5 ft 9 in) and 80 kg, he was never going to be a strong defender like Farrell; he preferred to get the ball and go, playing fast, attacking rugby on the run. That was the style he played for his club, Harlequins, where he won the 2021 Premiership Rugby final, but

England preferred to play a different way.

For the 2023 Men's Rugby World Cup, England coach Steve Borthwick had an idea: why not use Marcus' attacking skills as a full-back instead? He had been working hard on his speed and acceleration with former Olympic gold medallist Daley Thompson, and he showed it off by scoring two tries against Chile.

When Farrell decided to take a break from international rugby after the World Cup, Marcus moved back to fly-half for the 2024 Six Nations, and he calmly kicked a last-minute drop goal to win the game against Ireland. But is fly-half really his best position? For the 2025 Six Nations, Fin Smith was England's first-choice number 10, with Marcus back at full-back, and the two Smiths shone brightly together, while sharing the kicking duties. Because wherever he plays, Marcus always performs like a superstar.

"Magic Marcus" makes amazing things happen. I've interviewed him a few times pitchside when I've been a pundit. He wants to be the best and that drive to keep improving is infectious.

ENTERTAINER

FINN RUSSELL
FLY-HALF

POSITION **FLY-HALF**

DATE OF BIRTH **23 SEPTEMBER 1992**

COUNTRY **SCOTLAND**

CLUBS **FALKIRK, AYR, GLASGOW WARRIORS, RACING 92, BATH**

SUPERSTAR MOMENT **HELPING SCOTLAND TO BEAT ENGLAND IN 2018, FOR THE FIRST TIME IN 10 YEARS**

FUN FACT **FINN COMES FROM A BIG SPORTING FAMILY. HIS GRANDPARENTS WERE INTERNATIONAL BADMINTON PLAYERS, AND HIS UNCLE AND GREAT-GRANDFATHER BOTH PLAYED CRICKET FOR SCOTLAND.**

FINN RUSSELL

"Some people might say I'm good to watch. If you're a football fan you might say kinda like Messi." From any other rugby player, that might sound like the most arrogant thing ever, but from Finn Russell? Well, what else would you expect from the game's greatest entertainer?

Finn has always been a bit different. At the age of nineteen, when most stars were already playing professional club rugby, Finn was busy training to become a stonemason (a person who works on buildings made of stone), while also playing for Falkirk in Scotland's second division.

As his coach soon told him, Finn was too good, so he joined Glasgow Warriors in 2012, and just two magical years later, he was playing international rugby!

As Scotland's new number 10, Finn was following in the footsteps of his Glasgow coach, Gregor Townsend. Townsend was known as a skilful, attacking fly-half, and Finn was ready to carry on that tradition, although in his own unique way.

You see, Finn loves to kick, but not just to move

his team up the pitch, or to clear the danger in defence. Boring! No, he uses his kicks to create chances in attack. Kicks played out wide to the wingers, kicks chipped through the middle into gaps, even kicks poked through poor defenders' legs. Nutmeg!

And Finn is just as clever and skilful with his hands, too. Dainty dummies, outrageous offloads, long, looping passes – he'll try absolutely anything on the rugby pitch. If it doesn't work, oh well, never mind, he never worries too much about his mistakes. But if it works, wow, he looks like an absolute genius!

For example, during the British and Lions tour of South Africa in 2021, Finn came back from injury to completely change the game in the third Test. Not only did he score three penalties and a conversion, but he also got his team playing fast, flowing, exciting rugby. Afterwards, former England player Matt Dawson said, "If he was an All Black, you'd be saying he's the next Dan Carter – he's that good."

Like all the best Scots, Finn also seems to save his best performances for games against England. In the 2018 Six Nations, his risky but brilliant pass from deep in his own half helped set up a try as

Scotland claimed the Calcutta Cup for the first time in 10 years. A year later, the game was tied at 31–31 with minutes to go when Finn got the ball and delivered a beautiful no-look pass to fool the England defence and send Sam Johnson through to score (although England came back to draw). Then during the 2025 Six Nations, Finn had the chance to be Scotland's England-defeating hero again, but unfortunately, this time he missed his last-minute, match-winning conversion.

So, what's stopping Finn from becoming a Dan Carter-level superstar? Well, he always works hard on the pitch, but off it? Not so much. "I'm a rugby player, a fly-half, not a bodybuilder," he argues. "I love burgers and pizza too much, anyway."

Another funny quote from the game's greatest entertainer.

> **MAGGIE'S INSIGHTS**
> You can't help but feel a sense of joy while watching Finn because he always plays with a smile on his face. A brilliant fly-half who is not afraid to take risks and try things that many others wouldn't even think of attempting.

★ LEGEND ★

JOHNNY SEXTON
FLY-HALF

POSITION **FLY-HALF**

DATE OF BIRTH **11 JULY 1985**

COUNTRY **IRELAND**

CLUBS **LEINSTER, RACING MÉTRO 92**

SUPERSTAR MOMENT **WINNING A SIX NATIONS GRAND SLAM, THE EUROPEAN RUGBY CHAMPIONS CUP, AND THE WORLD RUGBY MEN'S PLAYER OF THE YEAR AWARD – ALL IN 2018!**

FUN FACT **HE'S A MASSIVE FAN OF MANCHESTER UNITED FOOTBALL CLUB AND GOT TO MEET THEIR FAMOUS FORMER MANAGER SIR ALEX FERGUSON IN 2021.**

JOHNNY SEXTON

From the flair of Finn Russell, to one of rugby's most competitive and consistent performers. Instead of a smile, Johnny Sexton usually played the game with a fierce glare, plus a lot of loud, angry words. But while he could be a nightmare to play with, he was always a nightmare to play against!

Johnny grew up in Dublin, Ireland, where he played rugby for Bective Rangers, and then for his school, St Mary's College. That's where he first caught the eye, by scoring a last-minute drop goal to win the Leinster Senior Schools Cup. There would be plenty more of those in the years to come...

By the age of 20, Johnny was already playing fly-half for Leinster, but another four years went by before he made his Ireland debut in 2009, against Fiji. And despite winning Player of the Match after scoring seven kicks out of seven, and then scoring all 15 points as they beat South Africa a week later, Johnny still didn't get to stay in the Ireland starting line-up. When the 2010 Six Nations came around, Ronan O'Gara was back wearing the number 10 shirt.

Oh well, Johnny kept working hard and kicking well whenever he got the chance, until eventually in 2012, he won the battle of the Irish fly-halves. Then, once the number 10 shirt was officially his, he took his game to an even higher level.

Johnny is best known for his incredible kicking, but he was also strong, skilful and fearless in defence, and also in attack. In 2013, he scored a try against Australia that helped the British and Irish Lions to their first series win since 1997. And when Ireland won the Six Nations in 2014, he scored four tries, as well as 18 kicks.

In 2016, Johnny suffered a series of nasty injuries, but he showed the resilience to bounce back for his two best years of all:

2018

Johnny started the year by scoring a last-minute drop goal against France to set Ireland on their way to winning a Six Nations Grand Slam, and he finished it by lifting the World Rugby Men's Player of the Year award. Oh, and in the middle, he also won the European Rugby Champions Cup with Leinster and helped Ireland beat the All Blacks!

2023

In his final year in international rugby, Johnny broke two Six Nations records: first for being the championship's oldest player (at 37!), and then, more importantly, for being the Championship's all-time leading points-scorer (beating O'Gara again!). Plus, he did it in the final game against England, firing Ireland to another Grand Slam!

So, could Johnny go on and complete an incredible career by also winning the 2023 Men's Rugby World Cup as Ireland captain? No. Unfortunately, Ireland lost to New Zealand in the quarter-finals, but as Johnny walked off with his usual angry frown, his young son Luca turned it upside down, saying "You're still the best, Dad." *Awwww!*

Despite the weight and pressure on his shoulders in captaining and representing his country, he always made it look effortless. He had a competitive mindset and he always expected high standards from himself and his teammates.

JONNY WILKINSON
FLY-HALF

POSITION **FLY-HALF**

DATE OF BIRTH **25 MAY 1979**

COUNTRY **ENGLAND**

CLUBS **NEWCASTLE FALCONS, TOULON**

SUPERSTAR MOMENT **SCORING THE WINNING DROP GOAL IN THE 2003 MEN'S RUGBY WORLD CUP FINAL**

FUN FACT **HIS GRANDFATHER PLAYED FOOTBALL FOR NORWICH CITY!**

★ GAMECHANGER ★

JONNY WILKINSON

Our final fly-half is most famous for being England's 2003 Men's Rugby World Cup hero, but he also helped put the "professional" in "professional rugby".

Even as a youngster, Jonny Wilkinson was fully focused on becoming a superstar. Aged eight, he wrote a list of future goals, which included "to be the kicker, to play for England, to win the World Cup, to be the best there was."

When he got a bit older, he would wake up early and practice kicking with both feet for 90 minutes before school. They say "practice makes perfect", and that's exactly what Jonny was aiming for: perfection. His robot-like routine would become world-famous: tapping his toes behind him, cupping his hands together in front of him, then bending his legs and *BANG! ... BALL STRAIGHT BETWEEN THE POSTS!*

As well as his kicking, Jonny also spent hours practising his passing, tackling, and reading of the game, until aged eighteen, he signed for Newcastle Falcons. By the end of his first season, Newcastle were the Premiership Champions and Jonny was already an England international!

In his first full game for his country against Australia in June 1998, Jonny missed some easy penalties, and England lost 76–0, but he refused to let one bad game ruin everything. Instead, he did what he did best: practised towards perfection.

With his kicking much improved, Jonny quickly became his country's superstar fly-half. When England beat South Africa in 2000, Jonny scored all 27 points! When England won a Six Nations Grand Slam in 2003, Jonny scored nearly half of the team's total points. He was all set for his biggest moment: the 2003 Men's Rugby World Cup.

In the quarter-finals against Wales, Jonny scored 23 points, and in the semi-finals against France, he scored all of England's 24 points, including three drop goals! But amazingly, he saved his best performance of all for the final against Australia...

In the first 80 minutes, Jonny kicked four high-pressure penalties (including one from 50 yards), and showed off his awesome all-round game: his strong tackling in defence, his skilful passing in attack, and his energetic running all over the field.

Then in extra-time, he delivered the greatest moment in England rugby history. With 99 minutes on the clock and a penalty shoot-out looming,

Jonny caught the ball, and – BANG! – with his weaker right foot, he calmly kicked a drop goal ... STRAIGHT BETWEEN THE POSTS!

Hurray, all those endless hours of practice had been worth it – thanks to him, England had just won the Men's Rugby World Cup for the first time ever!

Suddenly, shy, quiet Jonny was one of the world's biggest sporting superstars, and for the next few years, he really struggled with injuries and his mental health. But back he came to win two Heineken Cups with his club, Toulon, and to play at two more World Cups with his country, even becoming the tournament's all-time leading scorer.

Jonny was a fantastic fly-half who made history for England, but it was his professional approach that changed the game for ever.

MAGGIE'S INSIGHTS

What a historic moment! I remember watching the 2003 final with my England teammates, and it really inspired us to keeping trying to win the Women's Rugby World Cup. Since then, I've had the pleasure of working with Jonny as a broadcaster and even a temporary bodyguard when there's a sea of fans waiting for him!

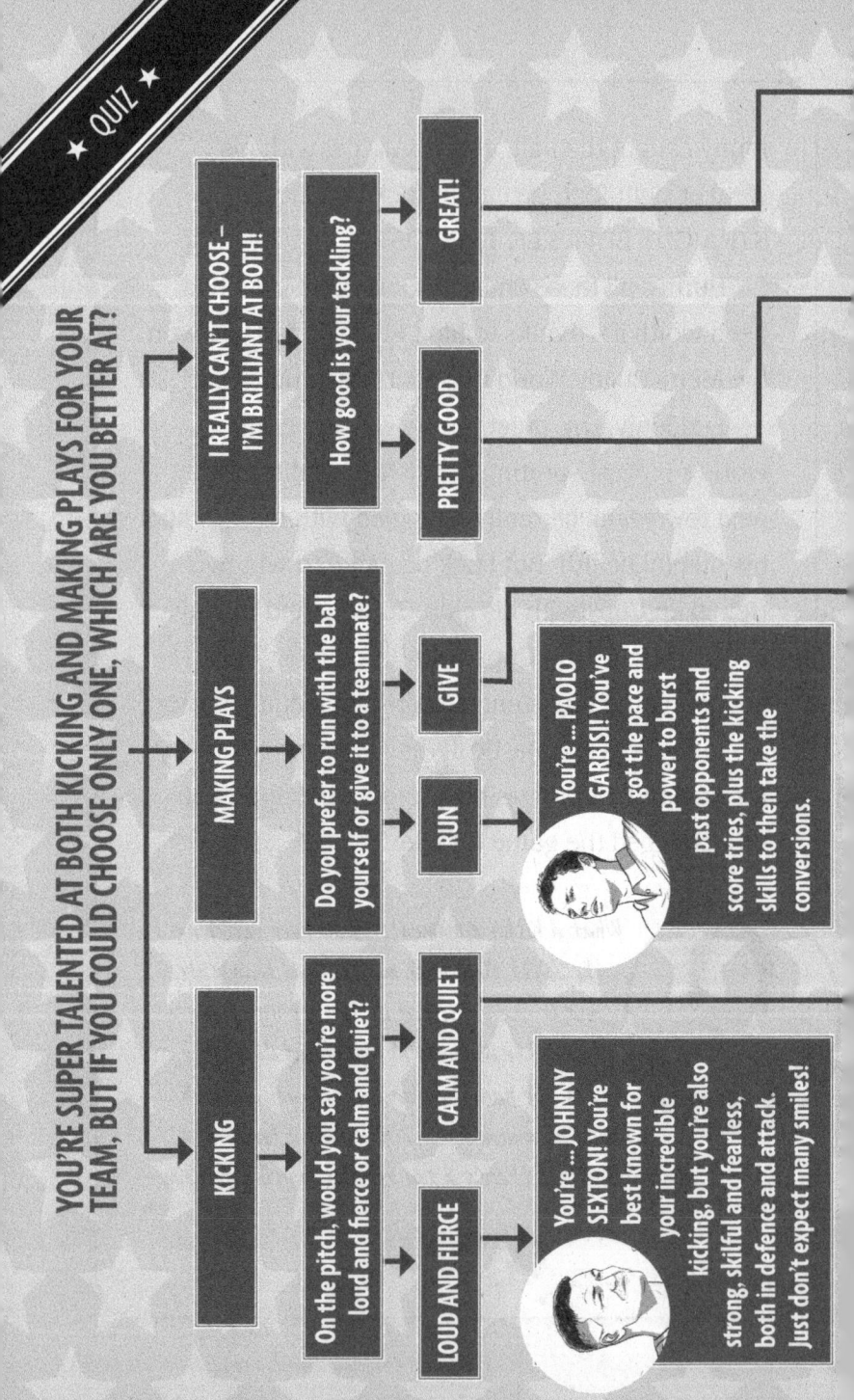

You spot a gap in the opposition defence: do you play a simple pass or go for a clever kick?

→ **SIMPLE PASS**

→ **CLEVER KICK**

You're ... **MARCUS SMITH!** You always do your best, but you're never going to be the strongest of defenders. You prefer to get the ball and go, playing fast, attacking rugby on the run.

You're ... **DAN CARTER!** In attack and defence, you tick all the rugby boxes. You're the ultimate fly-half, fantastic in every way.

You're ... **ANNA RICHARDS!** You're the perfect playmaker, controlling the game and creating chance after chance for your teammates with your vision and passing.

You're ... **JONNY WILKINSON!** You prefer to do your talking with your brilliant boot! All those endless hours of practice have made you an excellent kicker, even in the most high-pressure situations.

You're ... **FINN RUSSELL!** Cheeky chips, cross-field kicks, nutmegs, dummies – you'll try absolutely anything on the rugby pitch, and with such skilful hands and feet, you often succeed!

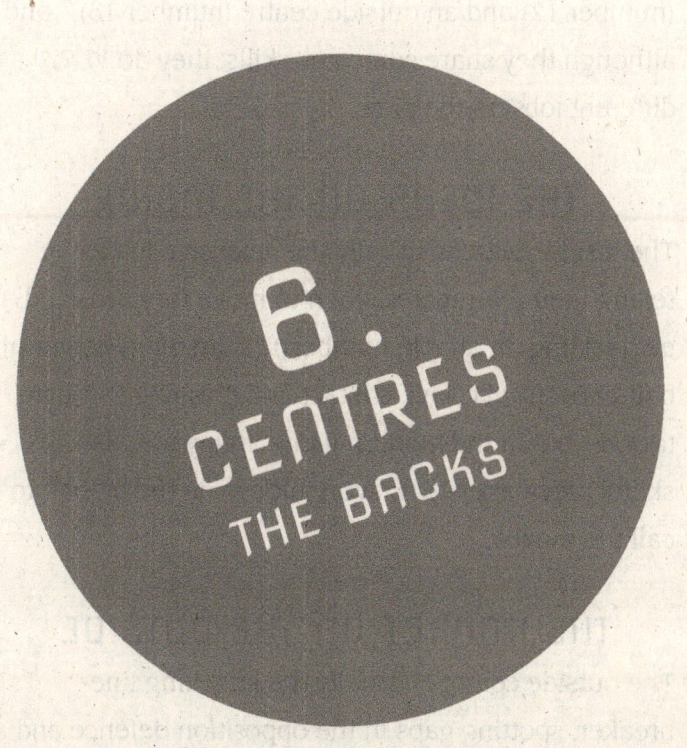

6. CENTRES
THE BACKS

We've got one more pair of backs in the middle to talk about ... the centres. But warning: while every team has two of them – an inside centre (number 12) and an outside centre (number 13) – and although they share some key skills, they do *VERY* different jobs on the pitch.

THE IDEAS ON THE INSIDE

The inside centre is usually the defensive leader, telling their teammates when to move forwards and get tackling. In attack, number 12s are often powerful ball-carriers who love contact and crashing through tackles, but in the modern game, many are also skilful playmakers who work alongside the fly-half to call the moves.

THE IMPACT ON THE OUTSIDE

The outside centre is usually the attacking line-breaker, spotting gaps in the opposition defence and bursting through them. From their wider position on the pitch, outside centres also help the fly-half to make decisions based on the spaces they see on the wings. Number 13s need to be able to read the game well in defence, too, knowing when to hold off, and when to commit to the crunching tackle.

TO BE A CENTRE SUPERSTAR YOU NEED:

1. Impressive passing

Centres play a crucial role in keeping an attacking move going and can assist in creating tries. They have to catch and pass the ball under pressure and pick the right pass for every situation. Their passes have to be accurate, so that they can either put a forward into a gap or release a winger waiting out wide.

2. Terrific tackling

The best centres are also strong tacklers. It's their role to defend the midfield and stop any ball-carriers breaking through because one missed tackle can ultimately result in a try. When defending, the centres need to work together and keep communicating.

3. Awesome acceleration

The best centres are quick off the mark. Inside centres need acceleration to break tackles and outside centres use it to burst through gaps in the opposition defence. When defending, both centres will use their acceleration to make powerful tackles to drive a player back, to pounce on a loose ball, or to hunt a player down who has just made a **line break**.

TO KICK OR NOT TO KICK?

Some centres are as skilful with their feet as they are with their hands:

STATS

- Although they are best known as fly-halves, **Jonny Wilkinson** and **Owen Farrell** both spent parts of their England careers playing at inside centre.
- **Emily Scarratt** has been one of England Women's main kickers since 2012 and is their all-time leading point-scorer.

Others are try-scoring machines:

- At the 2021 Women's Rugby World Cup, New Zealand's **Stacey Waaka** scored crucial tries in both the semi-final and the final.
- **Brian O'Driscoll** scored 46 Test tries, the most ever by a centre, and he's currently 9th on the all-time men's list.

VERY VERSATILE

Because they're so good in both defence and attack, centres are often used as a "utility back", which means they can play in lots of different positions:

🏉 New Zealand women's captain **Ruahei Demant** won the 2021 Women's Rugby World Cup as a fly-half, but has since moved to play inside centre for her country.

🏉 Although his favourite role is outside centre, **Elliot Daly** has also played at fly-half, full-back, and on the wing for England since making his debut in 2016!

A few very special centres have even had the all-round skills to play international rugby as both forwards AND backs:

🏉 Scotland international **Richie Vernon** went to the 2011 Men's Rugby World Cup as a number 8, but by the next tournament four years later, he had switched to become an outside centre!

🏉 **Levani Botia** starred as an inside centre for Fiji at the Men's Rugby World Cups in 2015 and 2019, but at the tournament in 2023, he played as a flanker instead!

CENTRES THEN ...

In the old days, the centres were usually more focused on attacking rather than defending, and so size and power were not so important. Legends of the game like Wales' Bleddyn Williams (1947–55) and France's Philippe Sella (1982–95) were much closer to the height (1.80 m) and weight (84 kg) of most modern fly-halves.

... V. CENTRES NOW

These days, defending is a key part of a centre's game, too, both in the tackle and at the breakdown. This means many are as big and strong as back rowers. Wales' Jamie Roberts (2008–17), for example, is 1.96 metre (6 ft 5 in) tall and weighs 107 kg, while England's Manu Tuilagi (2011–24) weighs even more! These modern centres aren't just massive monsters, though – they also have skilful hands and lightning-fast feet.

SO, WHICH KIND OF CENTRE WOULD YOU BE?

Will you kick like a fly-half, or weave your way to the try line like a winger? Will you be best known for your speed or skill, passing or power, defence or attack? Or maybe you're aiming to be the superstar centre who can do it all!

To help you decide, here's a look at some of the greatest centres rugby has ever seen, all with different styles and approaches. Then take our quiz to find out which superstar you would be.

★ LEGEND ★

BRIAN O'DRISCOLL
CENTRE

POSITION **OUTSIDE CENTRE (NO. 13)**

DATE OF BIRTH **21 JANUARY 1979**

COUNTRY **IRELAND**

CLUB **LEINSTER**

SUPERSTAR MOMENT **CAPTAINING IRELAND TO A SIX NATIONS GRAND SLAM IN 2009, FOR THE FIRST TIME IN 61 YEARS**

FUN FACT **AMAZINGLY, BRIAN PLAYED THE FIRST 10 YEARS OF HIS PROFESSIONAL RUGBY CAREER WITH ONLY 50 PER CENT OF THE AVERAGE PERSON'S UNAIDED VISION. HIS EYE CONDITION WAS ONLY FIXED WITH LASER TREATMENT IN 2009.**

BRIAN O'DRISCOLL

His nickname rhymes with "God" for a reason: that's how Brian O'Driscoll is seen by many rugby fans, especially in Ireland. For fifteen years between 1999 and 2014, "In BOD we trust" was the motto of the national team and his club, Leinster, and he never let his teams down.

As a kid growing up in Dublin, Brian started off playing Gaelic football, but really, he was always destined to play rugby. After all, the sport ran in the family; his dad had been an Ireland international, and so had two of his cousins!

With his kicking skills, Brian started out as a fly-half at school, but when he got to University College Dublin, he was asked to play as a centre instead.

Really? At 1.75 metres (5 ft 9 in), Brian was pretty small for a centre, but what he lacked in size, he always made up for in courage and commitment. In defence, he was brilliant at winning turnovers and intercepting passes. And in attack? He was brilliant at bursting through tackles!

In 1998, Brian won the Under-19 Men's Rugby World Cup with Ireland, and from there, he was on a fast-track to the top. Aged twenty, he made his debut for the senior team; aged 21, he scored a hat-trick of tries against France; aged 22, he scored a sensational solo try for the British and Irish Lions against Australia; and by 23, he was already the captain of his country!

So, could BOD lead Ireland to glory, after decades of disappointment? At the 2007 Men's Rugby World Cup, they suffered a surprise defeat to Argentina in the group stage and exited the tournament early, and in the Six Nations, they kept finishing second: in 2001, 2003, 2004, 2006, 2007…

But at last, in 2009, Ireland secured a first-place finish, and they did it in style, winning a Grand Slam for the first time since 1948. And who was named Player of the Tournament for the third time in four years? Yep, BOD, their captain and superstar centre!

That Six Nations, Brian was everywhere for Ireland; scoring crucial tries against France, Italy, England and Wales at one end, and then stopping them at the other with tremendous, last-chance tackles. What a hero!

And there was still plenty more of Brian's brilliance to come. As his super-speed began to fade, his smart rugby brain took over, and he went on to win three Heineken Cups with Leinster, play at one more World Cup and on two more Lions tours, and win another Six Nations Championship with Ireland in his final international match.

"It's great to finish on a high in my last game in this magnificent jersey," he said afterwards.

As well as two Six Nations titles, Brian also retired from international rugby with two very important personal records. His 46 Test tries made him the highest-scoring a) Irishman and b) centre of all time. What a legend!

MAGGIE'S INSIGHTS

As a young player, I used to be an inside centre (number 12), and even though Brian was an outside centre (number 13), I still grew up wanting to play like him. After his try for the Lions in 2001, we all wanted to be BOD! Two years later, aged nineteen, I made my international debut for England at inside centre versus the USA, and I made a break through their backs and crossed the try line to score. It was the best feeling and I owe Brian for showing me how it's done!

LEGEND

TANA UMAGA
CENTRE

POSITION **OUTSIDE CENTRE (NO. 13)**

DATE OF BIRTH **27 MAY 1973**

COUNTRY **NEW ZEALAND**

CLUBS **WELLINGTON, HURRICANES, TOULON, COUNTIES MANUKAU, CHIEFS**

SUPERSTAR MOMENT **LEADING NEW ZEALAND TO VICTORY OVER THE BRITISH AND IRISH LIONS IN 2005**

FUN FACT **AFTER RETIRING FROM RUGBY, TANA TOOK UP MARTIAL ARTS AND IS NOW A BLACK BELT IN BRAZILIAN JIU JITSU!**

TANA UMAGA

The very best centres are as brilliant in the tackle as they are on the run, and that's certainly true of our next superstar, Tana Umaga.

Growing up in Wellington, New Zealand's capital city, there was no question which sport Tana (short for Jonathan) would play. "At primary school most of my friends played soccer, but my dad wouldn't let me. He made me play rugby instead." The only question was: which kind of rugby would he play?

At first, Tana chose rugby league, and he even represented the Under-20 national team in 1991. But inspired by the style and success of the All Blacks, he decided to switch to rugby union a few years later.

With his ferocious power and speed, Tana started out as a winger for Wellington, and after scoring a record twelve tries in 1997, he got the call-up he had been hoping for: hurray, he was about to become an All Black!

It was a dream come true for Tana to play alongside the legendary Jonah Lomu, and at the 1999 Men's Rugby World Cup, they caused chaos together on the wings for New Zealand. Tana scored two tries in the quarter-finals against Scotland, but after losing to France in the semis, the All Blacks decided it was time to try something different. What about moving Tana to outside centre?

New position? No problem! As much as he loved to attack, Tana also loved to defend, and at centre, his job was to do both. Perfect! By the time the 2003 Men's Rugby World Cup came around, he was one of the best number 13s in the world, but just when he was at the peak of his powers, disaster struck. In the very first match against Italy, Tana suffered a tournament-ending knee injury, and without him, New Zealand fell at the semi-final stage again.

Tana bounced back brilliantly, though, and in 2004, he became the new All Blacks captain, plus their first-ever captain of Pacific Island heritage (his parents are from Samoa). His first task: to lead the Haka, the famous Māori dance that the players do before every match, and Tana even introduced a special new version called "Kapa o Pango" ("Team in Black").

His second, much bigger task was to lead New Zealand to victory over the British and Irish Lions in 2005. The tour started badly for Tana when his dangerous tackle injured his fellow centre legend, Brian O'Driscoll, but it ended excellently, with two bursting tries in the Third Test.

New Zealand won all three matches, and a total of 19 out of 21 under Tana's leadership. At the start of 2006, however, he suddenly announced that he was retiring from international rugby, at the age of just 32. One of the game's most fearsome players was gone, but certainly not forgotten.

MAGGIE'S INSIGHTS

A legend and a personal hero of mine. I used to love watching him play for the All Blacks. He read the game incredibly well; defensively he would always be in the right place at the right time. When at his best, he always cut great lines and made wonderful offloads to set up an attacking play.

TOMMASO MENONCELLO
CENTRE

- POSITION **INSIDE CENTRE (NO. 12)**
- DATE OF BIRTH **20 AUGUST 2002**
- COUNTRY **ITALY**
- CLUBS **BENETTON TREVISO**
- SUPERSTAR MOMENT **WINNING THE 2024 SIX NATIONS PLAYER OF THE CHAMPIONSHIP AWARD**
- FUN FACT **HE HAS A TATTOO ON HIS ARM OF THE NUMBER 717. WHY? BECAUSE HE WAS THE 717TH MAN TO PLAY RUGBY FOR ITALY.**

RISING STAR

TOMMASO MENONCELLO

From the rugby past to the rugby future: Tommaso Menoncello wasn't even born when Italy first joined the Six Nations back in 2000, but boy has he made a bright start in the tournament.

Tommaso made his Italy debut as a speedy winger against France in 2022, and in only the seventeenth minute, he became the youngest-ever try-scorer in Six Nations history, aged nineteen years and 170 days!

By the 2024 Six Nations, however, Tommaso had become a top international inside centre. He was sensational for Italy, winning Player of the Match against France, and even being named the Player of the Championship.

Tommaso carried his top form over into the 2025 tournament. He scored two tries, made more breakdown steals than any other back, and got shortlisted for the best player award again!

Tommaso caught everyone's eye in the 2024 Six Nations. His power, strength and pace are what make him a future talent.

★ MODERN HERO ★

JONATHAN DANTY
CENTRE

POSITION **INSIDE CENTRE (NO. 12)**

DATE OF BIRTH **7 OCTOBER 1992**

COUNTRY **FRANCE**

CLUBS **STADE FRANÇAIS, LA ROCHELLE**

SUPERSTAR MOMENT **WINNING THE SIX NATIONS GRAND SLAM WITH FRANCE IN 2022**

FUN FACT **HE'S A BIG BASKETBALL FAN AND HAS AN IMPRESSIVE COLLECTION OF NBA JERSEYS.**

JONATHAN DANTY

Jonathan Danty is an inside centre who looks like a flanker! But when he gets the ball, he can fly!

Jonathan made his France debut in 2016, but it wasn't until 2021 that he became his country's first-choice number 12, forming a successful new centre partnership with Gaël Fickou.

During the 2022 Six Nations, Jonathan was a monster in defence, winning tackles and turnovers, and an important player in attack, too. He powered his way to the try line against Scotland, and after one last win over England, France were crowned Grand Slam Champions!

Jonathan couldn't wait to shine for his country again, at the 2023 Men's Rugby World Cup in France. He started in style with two tries against Namibia, but unfortunately, France lost to South Africa in the quarter-finals ... by one single point!

Since then, injuries have slowed Jonathan's progress, but he's still a rugby force to be feared.

Jonathan is big, strong, and he only knows one direction and that's route one, straight into the opposition!

★ MODERN HERO ★

EMILY SCARRATT
CENTRE

POSITION **MOSTLY OUTSIDE CENTRE (NO. 13), BUT CAN PLAY ANYWHERE, REALLY!**

DATE OF BIRTH **8 FEBRUARY 1990**

COUNTRY **ENGLAND**

CLUBS **LICHFIELD, LOUGHBOROUGH LIGHTNING**

SUPERSTAR MOMENT **SCORING THE WINNING TRY IN THE 2014 WOMEN'S RUGBY WORLD CUP FINAL**

FUN FACT **MOST PEOPLE IN RUGBY CALL HER BY HER NICKNAME: "SCAZ"!**

EMILY SCARRATT

A World Cup winner, the 2019 Women's World Player of the Year, an eight-time Women's Six Nations winner, and England Women's all-time record point-scorer since 2020 – Emily Scarratt is already a rugby legend, but because she's still playing and starring for the Red Roses, we'll stick with modern hero for now.

Growing up in Leicester, Emily was excellent at every sport she tried. She played hockey for her county, rounders for England, and she was even offered a scholarship to go and play basketball in the USA! But in the end, rugby was the sport Emily loved best.

One day, aged five, she was watching her brother play, when a coach asked if she'd like to join in. "Yes please!" she said, and after that, there was no stopping her. When she wasn't scoring tries, she was practising her kicking on the family farm, using goalposts made from bales of hay and a scaffolding pole!

Emily's childhood rugby hero was Leicester's Geordan Murphy, and she was also inspired by athletes Kelly Holmes and Cathy Freeman. "It was incredible watching physically strong women doing amazing things on the world stage," she says. "But I didn't know women could play rugby at an elite level."

By the time she was eighteen, however, Emily was already playing for England. In her first year, she scored twelve tries in twelve games as a full-back, and she turned out to be even better as a centre. After all, she was tall, fast, skilful and powerful.

At her first Women's Rugby World Cup in 2010, Emily experienced the high of scoring against the USA, followed by the low of losing to New Zealand in the final (which would happen again in 2017 and 2021). Never mind, she was still young, with plenty of time to make things right…

By the 2014 Women's Rugby World Cup, Emily was playing better than ever, and she was also now England's first-choice kicker. She scored twenty points against Samoa, fifteen against Spain, and eleven against Ireland to fire her team to another final.

Against Canada, Emily scored sixteen of England's 21 points, including a wonderful World Cup-winning try! After bursting through one tackle, she then weaved through five more defenders, before diving over the line. What a moment –

England were the new World Champions!

With that mission accomplished, Emily set off for a new challenge in rugby sevens. But after helping Team GB finish fourth at the 2016 Olympics, and then win the Bronze Medal at the 2018 Commonwealth Games, she returned to her first loves: rugby union and the Red Roses.

In 2020, Emily was named the Women's Six Nations Player of the Tournament as England won a Grand Slam; in 2022, she won her 100th cap in front of a loud home crowd in Leicester, and the caps, points and incredible performances just keep coming!

So, what's Emily's greatest strength as a centre? Apparently, that's a hard question to answer. "She can run, pass, kick, catch, high-ball catch, everything," says her England coach Simon Middleton!

MAGGIE'S INSIGHTS

There is nothing this player can't do. Thankfully, I had the privilege to play alongside "Scaz" and compete at two World Cups with her. She was excellent in 2010, but in 2014, she was simply unstoppable, especially in the final against Canada, as we took the trophy home for the first time in 20 years!

★ ENTERTAINER ★

SEMI RADRADRA
CENTRE

POSITION **OUTSIDE CENTRE (NO. 13)**

DATE OF BIRTH **13 JUNE 1992**

COUNTRY **FIJI**

CLUBS **TOULON, BORDEAUX BÈGLES, BRISTOL BEARS, LYON**

SUPERSTAR MOMENT **HIS STUNNING PERFORMANCE AGAINST WALES AT THE 2019 MEN'S RUGBY WORLD CUP**

FUN FACT **SEMI IS ALSO A BEAUTIFUL SINGER – THERE'S A VIDEO OF HIM ON YOUTUBE.**

SEMI RADRADRA

If you're looking for strong, speedy centres who destroy defenders for fun, then Semi Radradra is the flair player for you!

Semi grew up on the South Pacific island country of Fiji, playing rugby with his friends every day. "We would just grab whatever we could find – an empty plastic bottle or a coconut – and use it as a ball after school," he says.

But while Semi dreamed of becoming a superstar, it didn't seem possible. Fiji was not one of the big rugby nations, and he came from a farming family who needed him to start earning money. So aged sixteen, Semi went off to work in a dangerous gold mine.

"It was hard but it shaped me," he says. "A few months later, I was selected with the Fiji Under-20s and my life changed."

At the 2011 International Rugby Board (IRB) Junior World Championship, Semi shone brightly, scoring two tries against Tonga. With his speed, skill, size and strength, he was all set to become a superstar, but was rugby union really the right sport for him?

First, Semi tried rugby sevens, and then a year later, an Australian rugby league team signed him up, based only on a photo of his powerful legs! Semi had never watched, let alone played, rugby league, but the Parramatta Eels told him, "We'll teach you."

Semi successfully became a rugby league superstar, but in 2017, he joined French rugby union side Toulon. So, could he shine for Fiji again, just like he had in rugby sevens and rugby league?

The answer was a big, strong "YES!" Semi scored as Fiji beat France for the first time ever, and then at the 2019 Men's Rugby World Cup, he was the tournament's breakout star. Semi scored two magical tries against Georgia, and then against Wales he won the Player of the Match award, even though Fiji lost! The wicked sidestep, the sudden acceleration, the outrageous offloads – Semi was a joy to watch and simply unstoppable. In total, he beat 29 defenders, more than any other player at the World Cup, despite playing only four games!

Rugby union's new exciting superstar joined Bristol Bears from Bordeaux Bègles in 2020, where he carried on entertaining by:

- hopping over the try line on one leg against Clermont (he had injured the other!),
- weaving his way through the whole Bath team to score,
- and setting up a try against Zebre Parma with an unbelievable round-the-back pass.

But Semi doesn't just play for fun; he plays to win. He helped Bristol lift the Challenge Cup in 2020, and finish top of the Premiership in 2021, while at the 2023 Men's Rugby World Cup, his Fiji team beat Australia and qualified for the knockout stage for the first time since 2007.

Semi is an inspiration to anyone with a life goal: "I dreamt that I would be playing rugby out there in the world someday. I knew that if I kept my head down, kept working hard and believing in myself, I could get to the top."

MAGGIE'S INSIGHTS

It's never a dull game when Semi is playing. Every time he has the ball, you feel like he is going to make something happen. If you love watching free-flowing rugby — and lots of amazing late offloads — then he's definitely the player for you!

★ GAMECHANGER ★

GABRIELLE VERNIER
CENTRE

POSITION **INSIDE CENTRE (NO. 12)**

DATE OF BIRTH **12 JUNE 1997**

COUNTRY **FRANCE**

CLUBS **LILLE MRCV, BLAGNAC**

SUPERSTAR MOMENT **WINNING THE 2023 WOMEN'S SIX NATIONS PLAYER OF THE CHAMPIONSHIP AWARD**

FUN FACT **AWAY FROM RUGBY, GABRIELLE ENJOYS TRAVELLING AND SURFING.**

GABRIELLE VERNIER

In rugby, people often think the bigger you are, the better you are, but one outstanding performance at a time, France's Gabrielle Vernier is changing minds and changing the women's game.

At 1.65 metres (5 ft 5 in) and 65 kg, she is usually one of the smallest players on the pitch in any position, especially at centre, where opponents like Emily Scarratt (1.81 metres or 5 ft 11 in), tower over her. Does Gabrielle let that bother her, though? Not one bit!

"I was a fighter from a young age," she says. "I had to defend myself with two older brothers!"

It was those big brothers who first got Gabrielle into rugby, and aged ten, she began playing with the boys at Rueil Athletic Club, just west of Paris. From there, Gabrielle moved on to Racing Club Nanterre, and then up north to Lille, where she combined her university studies with playing rugby.

That might sound like a tricky balancing act, but Gabrielle made it look so easy. In 2016, she won the French Championship with Lille MRCV, and just two years later, she was part of the France squad that won the Women's Six Nations.

Back then, Gabrielle was best known as a tough-tackling defender, and at the 2021 Women's Rugby World Cup, she wowed the fans with big crunching stops on England stars Emily Scarratt and Ellie Kildunne, and New Zealand's Ruby Tui. Wow, how did someone so small hit so hard?

In France's semi-final defeat by New Zealand, Gabrielle also powered her way past flanker Alana Bremner (1.78 metres or 5 ft10 in, 77 kg) to score a try. It was a great show of strength, but more importantly, an exciting sign of things to come. Because as well as being a fearless defender, Gabrielle could also be an awesome attacker. She had the speed and nimble feet to burst past opponents, and she was small and smart enough to slip through gaps and out of tackles.

At the 2023 Six Nations, France finally unleashed their *fusée de poche* (that's "pocket rocket", in case you wondered!), and the results were spectacular: five tries in five games, plus a try-assist. Unfortunately, France lost the title decider against England, but there was no doubt who the Player of the Championship had been: Gabrielle!

"I was pleased to play with freedom at last," she said afterwards. "Those are things that I did a lot at club level and it's true that with France, until now, I felt less comfortable in attack."

At the 2024 Women's Six Nations, Gabrielle scored another great try against England, but again, her team lost the match they call Le Crunch (great name for the France v. England game, huh?!). France are getting closer and closer, though, and better and better, thanks to their small but mighty inside centre.

Don't let her size fool you; Gabrielle packs a punch. I remember watching her make a crunching tackle against England during the 2021 Women's Rugby World Cup. The tackle was so big you could feel the contact through the screen! She is a shining example that size doesn't matter.

★ QUIZ ★

WHICH TITLE DESCRIBES YOU BEST?

- **TRY-SCORING MACHINE**
  - If you had to play another rugby position, would you be a fly-half or a winger?
    - **FLY-HALF** → You're ... BRIAN O'DRISCOLL! Kicking? Defending? Creating chances for teammates? No problem, but you're best on the attack, bursting through tackles to score try after try.
    - **WINGER** →

- **MIDFIELD POWERHOUSE**
  - If you really had to choose between defending and attacking, which would you say you're best at?
    - **DEFENDING** →
    - **ATTACKING** →

- **ICE-COLD KICKER** → You're ... EMILY SCARRATT! You're the superstar centre who can do it all, but of all your weapons, your boot is the mightiest.

Would you say you're tall and speedy, or small and agile?

→ TALL AND SPEEDY
→ SMALL AND AGILE

You're … GABRIELLE VERNIER! Yes, you're a tough tackler, but you've also got the nimble feet to burst past opponents, and you're small and smart enough to slip through gaps and out of tackles.

You're … TOMMASO MENONCELLO! As much as you love a big, try-saving tackle, your game is more about bursting forwards, and using your pace and power on the attack.

You're … JONATHAN DANTY! Tackles, turnovers, steals at the breakdown – you're a monster in defence, and a real force to be feared. Plus, you're an important player in attack too, with your powerful running.

How do you feel about tackling?

→ IT'S OK
→ I LOVE IT!

You're … SEMI RADRADRA! You're all about attacking, and you've got the speed, strength and skill to get the ball, beat every defender, and score.

You're … TANA UMAGA! As much as you love to attack and score amazing tries, you also love to defend and make mighty tackles.

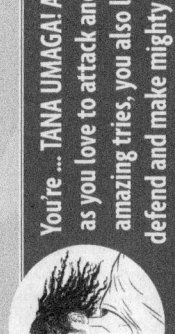

7. BACK THREE
THE BACKS

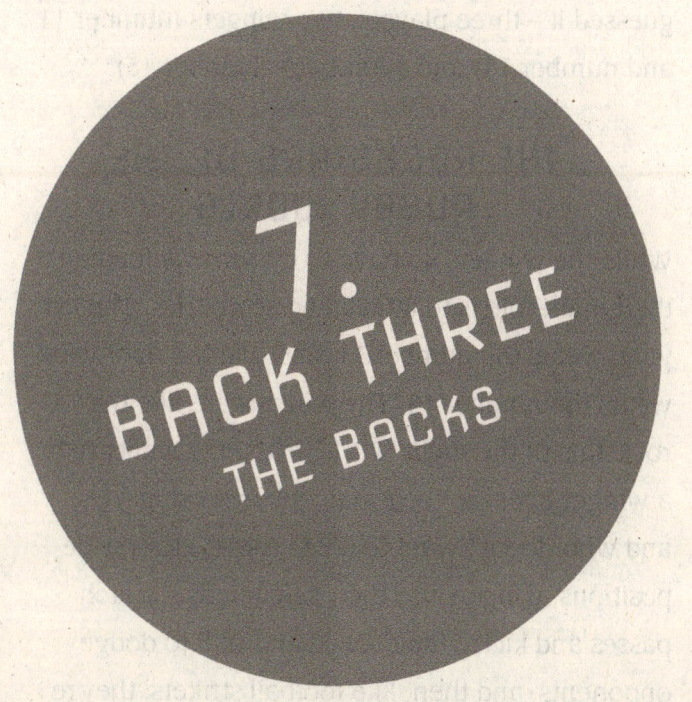

Right, we've reached the final section on the team sheet, and we've saved probably the most exciting set of rugby positions for last. Meet ... the back three! The back three is formed of – yep, you guessed it – three players: two wingers (number 11 and number 14) and a full-back (number 15).

THE ROCKSTARS OF THE RUGBY WORLD

While the wingers do have to do some defending, their main role is to attack and score tries. The left wing wears the number 11 shirt and the right wing wears the number 14. The wingers are like the rockstars of the rugby world; everyone wants to be a winger because their main job is scoring tries, and who doesn't want to score tries?! From wide positions, wingers use their safe hands to catch passes and kicks, their speed and skill to dodge opponents, and then, like football strikers, they're expected to be calm, confident finishers. It's not all about attacking, though; wingers must be top tacklers in defence, too, which means size and strength are also important.

LAST LINE OF DEFENCE, FIRST LINE OF ATTACK

The full-back wears number 15 and stands at the back of the field. Their main job is to be the last line of defence, so if a player from the opposition breaks through the backline, then they should be there to make that heroic, try-saving tackle. They also cover the backfield to deal with any kicks that come through or over their defence. It's not all about defending, though; full-backs must be dangerous attackers, too, whether running with the ball from deep, or moving forwards to join the other backs on a bursting break.

But despite their different roles, wingers and full-backs work closely together and have a lot in common.

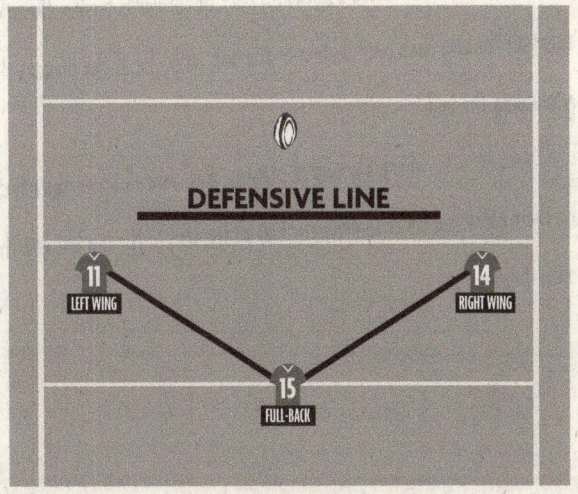

RUGBY RULES

SCORING A TRY

To score a TRY, a player must apply "downward pressure" to the ball — usually with a hand or arm, but the front of the body from waist to neck is also fine — as they touch (rather than drop or throw) it down beyond the try line. If the player's feet are on the ground as they do this, they must be on the pitch and not over the touchline.

When you hear the words "rugby try", most people think of a player weaving their way past lots of defenders and diving over the try line, but there are also two other, less beautiful ways to score:

- **FROM A SCRUM:** where a powerful pack of forwards pushes the other team all the way back over their own try line, with one of the players then grounding the ball.

- **FROM A MAUL:** where a group of players, this time all up on their feet, use their combined force to drive the ball all the way to the try line and then touch it down.

TO BE A BACK THREE SUPERSTAR YOU NEED:

1. Super speed

A back three superstar should be one of the fastest players on the field. It's the role of the players around them (especially the fly-half and centres) to get the ball to them in the best attacking position, and then – *ZOOM!* – away they go, using their electric pace to power them past opponents and all the way to the **try** line...

2. Magical movement

But it takes more than just super speed to become a try-scoring machine! The best wingers and full-backs are also great evaders, escaping from tackles with their fast, dancing feet, and bamboozling defenders with their beautiful sidesteps and swerves.

3. Terrific tackling

Being a back three superstar isn't all about scoring tries, though; sometimes, you've got to save them too! As the last line of defence before the try line, wingers and full-backs have to be good defenders as well as attackers. It's their job to jump up and catch high balls, to stop a line break or put their body on the line to make that last-ditch tackle.

TRY-SCORING SUPERSTARS

In most teams, the best attackers are members of the back three:

STATS

- Japan's **Daisuke Ohata** (1996–2006) is the all-time leading try-scorer in the men's international game with 69, followed by South Africa's **Bryan Habana** (67) and Australia's **David Campese** (64). They're all wingers!
- New Zealand winger **Portia Woodman** (2013–24) holds the record for most tries scored at the Women's World Cup: twenty!

THE BACK THREE THEN …

Believe it or not, it didn't really exist! No, in the old days of rugby, these players weren't grouped together like that; teams had a winger on each side of the pitch and the full-back was a totally separate position, where the player stood all alone at the very back as the last line of defence. In fact, in the early years of rugby, the full-back role was so defensive that it took over 50 years for the first full-back to finally score a try in the Five (now Six) Nations, in 1934!

... V. THE BACK THREE NOW

In modern rugby, the back three work together as a unit, in attack and defence, and so many players are comfortable switching between positions. One of the wingers has sprinted forwards, leaving a big empty space? No problem, the full-back will race across to cover. The full-back wants to get the ball and *goooooooo*? No problem, one of the wingers will just stay back instead!

SO, WHICH KIND OF BACK THREE SUPERSTAR WOULD YOU BE?

Will you be a tricky winger with turbo jets for feet, a brave full-back who's brilliant at catching high balls, or a back-three genius who can play both positions? Will you be all about attack, or do a great job in defence, too? And what will your try-scoring supertalent be: speed, skill, power, or a magical mix of all three?

To help you decide, here's a look at some of the greatest wingers and full-backs rugby has ever seen, all with different styles and approaches. Then take our quiz to find out which superstar you would be.

★ LEGEND ★

JONAH LOMU
BACK THREE

POSITION **WINGER**

DATE OF BIRTH **12 MAY 1975**

COUNTRY **NEW ZEALAND**

CLUBS **COUNTIES MANUKAU, BLUES, CHIEFS, HURRICANES, WELLINGTON, CARDIFF BLUES, NORTH HARBOUR, MARSEILLE VITROLLES**

SUPERSTAR MOMENT **DESTROYING ENGLAND AT THE 1995 MEN'S RUGBY WORLD CUP!**

FUN FACT **THERE ARE ONLY TWO TOP RUGBY NATIONS THAT JONAH NEVER SCORED AGAINST: SOUTH AFRICA (IN 12 MATCHES) AND WALES (IN 3 MATCHES).**

JONAH LOMU

Although Jonah Lomu's international rugby career lasted only eight years, his impact will last for ever, as the game's first global superstar.

Growing up in Auckland, New Zealand, Jonah had a talent for sport. Although he was an amazing all-round athlete – he once ran the 100 metres in 11.2 seconds – it was on the rugby pitch that he shone the brightest.

Because Jonah was so tall and strong, he started out in the back row, but what a waste of his super-speed! Eventually, his school coach moved him to the wing to give him more room to run, and that's when he really took off. Woah, who was this massive young winger destroying every defender who dared come near him? Jonah soon found himself flying through the New Zealand ranks. In a whirlwind 1994, he played for the Under-21s, the national rugby sevens team AND the All Blacks, all in one year!

Aged nineteen years and 45 days, Jonah became the youngest All Black ever, and less than a year later, he was blowing everyone away at the 1995 Men's Rugby World Cup. At that time, most wingers were small and speedy, but massive and mighty Jonah was on a mission to change the game. He scored two tries against Ireland, another against Scotland, and then a fantastic four in the semi-final against England!

ZOOM! – Jonah ran with the ball at breathtaking speed, and if a defender tried to tackle him ...

BOOM! – he bumped them off with ease, or ...

VROOM! – he fooled them with an extra burst of speed and a brilliant body swerve.

Yes, the wonderkid had skills, as well as pace and power – one journalist even described Jonah as a "freight train in ballet shoes"!

Although New Zealand lost to South Africa in the 1995 Men's Rugby World Cup final, Jonah was all set to become rugby's first real superstar, and what perfect timing, because the game was just turning professional. Suddenly, his face was everywhere, he was selling out stadiums, and he even had a PlayStation game named after him.

At the next Men's Rugby World Cup in 1999, Jonah broke his own record by scoring eight tries, but New Zealand again failed to lift the trophy. And sadly, before Jonah's third tournament in 2003, his explosive career came to an early end. After years of battling with a serious kidney problem, he was forced to retire from international rugby at the age of only 27. A few years later, he had a kidney transplant, but he died in 2015, aged 40.

Jonah's legacy lives on with the amazing All Blacks and the long list of big, powerful wingers who followed him, from Julian Savea to Duhan van der Merwe. In just eight years, 63 games and 37 tries, Jonah became a rugby icon and changed the game for ever.

A legend AND a gamechanger. Jonah was built like a forward with thighs the size of tree trunks and the power to break any tackle — but he also had the pace of a back. He transformed the way wingers played, and changed the entire sport.

★ LEGEND ★

BRYAN HABANA

BACK THREE

POSITION **WINGER**

DATE OF BIRTH **12 JUNE 1983**

COUNTRY **SOUTH AFRICA**

CLUBS **GOLDEN LIONS, BULLS, STORMERS, TOULON**

SUPERSTAR MOMENT **WINNING THE 2007 MEN'S RUGBY WORLD CUP WITH SOUTH AFRICA**

FUN FACT **BRYAN IS NAMED AFTER BRYAN ROBSON, A FORMER CAPTAIN OF MANCHESTER UNITED, THE FOOTBALL CLUB THAT HIS DAD, BERNIE, SUPPORTS.**

BRYAN HABANA

Next up we've got a winger so fast that he once raced a cheetah in a TV advert! Spoiler alert: he lost, but don't worry. Bryan Habana won pretty much everything else in his incredible rugby career.

Growing up in Johannesburg, his dad, Bernie, was a big rugby fan, but Bryan preferred cricket and football. That all changed, however, when he was eleven years old, and the Men's Rugby World Cup came to South Africa.

It was a massive moment for the country, and Bernie was so excited that he took Bryan out of school to watch the opening game together. South Africa won, and they ended up going back for the quarter-finals, the semi-finals, and then the final, where they watched their white captain Francois Pienaar lift the World Cup trophy presented by South Africa's Black president, Nelson Mandela. What an inspiring image! The next year, Bryan started playing rugby at school, dreaming that "one day I would be able to do the same, and hopefully be a part of a team that inspired a new generation".

As a small, skinny kid, Bryan began his rugby career as a scrum-half, but after a growth spurt, he moved onto the wing where he used his super-speed – he once ran the 100 m in 10.2 seconds – to score try after try for his school and then for his first professional club, the Golden Lions. Next step: the national team!

In 2004, aged 21, Bryan played his first game for South Africa against England, and with his very first touch off the bench, he caught the ball and sprinted through to score. What a dream debut! And after that, the tries kept coming: ten in his first ten matches, then fifteen in his first twenty...

Bryan arrived at the 2007 Men's Rugby World Cup as one of the game's biggest superstars, and he showed it, scoring four tries against Samoa, two against the USA, and then two more in the semi-final against Argentina. South Africa were through to another final, where they beat England to lift the trophy again. Wow, Bryan was a World Champion, just like he had imagined it as a boy back in 1995!

Bryan was named the 2007 World Rugby Men's Player of the Year, and over the next ten years, the big tries kept on coming, including a beautiful, weaving run to beat the British and Irish Lions in 2009, a hat-trick against Australia in 2012, and another hat-trick against the USA at the 2015 Men's

Rugby World Cup, where he also equalled Jonah Lomu's all-time tournament record of fifteen tries.

In 2018, Bryan retired from international rugby with 124 caps, the most won by any winger, and 67 tries, the most scored by any player from the top ten nations. His place in rugby history was secured as one of the greatest, and probably the fastest, winger to ever play the game.

MAGGIE'S INSIGHTS

Every time Bryan touched the ball, the crowd would go wild, because you knew something special could happen. He is a role model to many because, like Siya Kolisi, his story is inspiring and represents diversity and how, regardless of your start or background, you can still make it.

PORTIA WOODMAN

BACK THREE

POSITION **WINGER**

DATE OF BIRTH **12 JULY 1991**

COUNTRY **NEW ZEALAND**

CLUBS **AUCKLAND STORM, COUNTIES MANUKAU HEAT, NORTHLAND KAURI, CHIEFS MANAWA, BLUES WOMEN, MIE PEARLS**

SUPERSTAR MOMENT **WINNING THE 2017 AND 2021 WOMEN'S RUGBY WORLD CUPS WITH NEW ZEALAND**

FUN FACT **IN 2022, PORTIA MARRIED HER FELLOW BLACK FERNS WINGER RENEE WICKLIFFE, AND THEIR SURNAME BECAME WOODMAN-WICKLIFFE.**

PORTIA WOODMAN (NOW WOODMAN-WICKCLIFFE)

After watching a video of New Zealand versus England at the 1995 Men's Rugby World Cup, a nine-year-old Portia Woodman announced to her family, "I want to be the female Jonah Lomu!" Fast-forward 25 years, and we'd say she's completed that mission.

Portia's dad, Kawhena, and uncle, Fred, both played for the All Blacks in the 1980s, but for a girl growing up in the 1990s, the path to playing high-level rugby was far from clear, and so instead Portia focused on other sporting dreams.

"When I was younger, I wanted to be the fastest woman in the world, race at the Olympics in the 100-metre sprint," she remembers. Although she was a really good runner, Portia wasn't quite at the Olympic level, and so aged sixteen, she switched her focus to netball, and then back to rugby.

With rugby sevens becoming an Olympic sport in 2016, New Zealand launched a project in 2012, to build a hopefully Gold Medal-winning team and Portia signed up straight away!

At last, she had found her perfect sport, where she could combine the speed she had built through athletics, with the footwork and hand skills she had developed through netball. In 2013, Portia was the top scorer as New Zealand won the Rugby Sevens World Cup, and in 2015, she was named World Women's Rugby Sevens Player of the Year!

But after losing to Australia in the Gold Medal match at the 2016 Olympics, Portia decided to take a break from rugby sevens, and take on a new challenge with the Black Ferns, the New Zealand women's fifteen-a-side team.

Could Portia make a successful switch from rugby sevens to rugby union? Of course she could! At the 2017 Women's Rugby World Cup, she was unstoppable, using her pace, power and pure determination to weave through tackle after tackle. She scored eight tries in one match against Hong Kong, then four more in the semi-final against the USA, and when New Zealand beat England in the final, Portia became a World Champion in two different forms of the game!

Over the next seven years, she switched back and forth between the two, winning the top prize in everything:

- a Gold Medal in rugby sevens at the 2020 Olympics,
- the 2021 Women's Rugby World Cup (where she top-scored again with seven tries, while also becoming the tournament's all-time leading try-scorer),
- and another Gold Medal at the Olympic Games in 2024!

"I still feel like I'm a little netball player trying to play rugby sometimes," Portia says. But her incredible collection of trophies and awards says otherwise. It says that she's a true legend of the game.

MAGGIE'S INSIGHTS

I've watched and commentated on Portia over her career ... and wow, it's been some career! Not many players have made the switch between rugby sevens and fifteens successfully, but she is world-class in both. Her speed and power are unreal — you don't want to blink just in case you miss her. She has left a legacy that not many players will be able to emulate.

★ RISING STAR ★

ELLIE KILDUNNE
BACK THREE

POSITION **FULL-BACK**

DATE OF BIRTH **8 SEPTEMBER 1999**

COUNTRY **ENGLAND**

CLUBS **GLOUCESTER-HARTPURY, WASPS, HARLEQUINS**

SUPERSTAR MOMENT **WINNING THE 2024 WORLD RUGBY WOMEN'S PLAYER OF THE YEAR AWARD**

FUN FACT **IN 2024, ELLIE USED HER PASSION FOR FASHION TO DESIGN A CLOTHING RANGE FOR THE RED ROSES.**

ELLIE KILDUNNE

Can Ellie Kildunne count as a "rising star" when she's already won the World Rugby Women's Player of the Year award? We say yes, because England's flying full-back is still getting better and better!

As a young girl growing up in Yorkshire, Ellie played football, rugby league and rugby union every weekend. But aged fifteen, she chose to focus on rugby union, and three years later, she was making her debut for the Red Roses, the England senior team!

The only problem? Her coaches wanted her to play in a totally new position! Ellie had never been a full-back before, but despite a yellow card, a few missed tackles and some wild kicks, she came away from her first Test series against Canada with four tries.

Ellie clearly had lots of potential; now, she needed to improve her kicking, tackling and positioning in defence, to go with her excellent speed and step in attack. Luckily she had the chance to learn from one of the very best in the game: Danielle "Nolli" Waterman, England's full-back for the last fifteen years.

All that practice paid off as Ellie helped England win a 2020 Women's Six Nations Grand Slam, and then a year later, she scored the opening try in the Women's Rugby World Cup final, which England eventually lost against New Zealand.

Game by game, year by year, Ellie was getting better and better, but still, no one was expecting her to explode quite like she did at the 2024 Women's Six Nations. In England's first game against Italy, Ellie ran forwards to catch a high-ball and then danced her way through the defence. *TRY!* All of a sudden, she was flying at full-back, and she couldn't stop scoring. She got two tries against Italy, then two against Wales, and two more against Scotland!

Wow, Ellie was on fire, with six tries already in her first three matches, and against Ireland, she added three more – HAT-TRICK! Although she didn't score again in the title decider against France, Ellie still played her part in England's victory, and afterwards, she collected the Player of the Championship award. Then, six months later, she also picked up the 2024 World Rugby Women's Player of the Year prize, and a year later, she celebrated winning her 50th cap for England by scoring a hat-trick of tries against Wales in the 2025 Six Nations!

So, what's changed to turn Ellie into such a superstar? Well, she plays with way more power these days, thanks to lots of extra sessions in the gym. "I've gone through a wild journey to loving my strength and loving my muscles," she admits, "and understanding the benefits of being strong on the pitch and not just fast."

There's also Ellie's new superpower: her hair! "One day, I forgot my headband, and ended up playing with my hair down," she says, "and it gave me this mindset that I was way stronger, way faster."

What next for the rising star of women's rugby – winning another Six Nations and the 2025 Women's World Cup? Yes, but Ellie is also aiming even higher. "I want to be the best player in the world, man or woman," she says.

Ellie's pace, acceleration and ability to escape from tackles are the skills that set her apart from other players. She has an amazing future ahead of her.

★ MODERN HERO ★

DAMIAN PENAUD
BACK THREE

POSITION **WINGER**

DATE OF BIRTH **25 SEPTEMBER 1996**

COUNTRY **FRANCE**

CLUBS **CLERMONT, BORDEAUX BÈGLES**

SUPERSTAR MOMENT **WINNING THE 2022 SIX NATIONS GRAND SLAM WITH FRANCE**

FUN FACT **DUE TO A RUGBY INJURY, DAMIAN HAS FALSE FRONT TEETH. THERE'S A TIKTOK VIDEO OF HIM SCOOPING THEM UP OUT OF A CUP OF COFFEE AND INTO HIS MOUTH.**

DAMIAN PENAUD

A nickname like "the Phenomenon" is a lot to live up to, but Damian Penaud doesn't seem to feel the pressure. Whether he's playing for his club, Bordeaux Bègles, or his country, France, he's just a try-scoring machine!

Damian came through the rugby ranks at Brive, the team his dad had played for, but aged fifteen, he moved on to a bigger club, Clermont, where he made his way up from the academy to the first team. So, was Damian the kind of determined young player who spent hours practising after training? Hmm, no, not exactly – "He would arrive late to training, wearing flip-flops and with one eye still closed," says his former teammate Aurélien Rougerie. "He was ridiculously talented but he wasn't making the most of his opportunity."

With a bit of pushing, however, Damian's special talent began to shine through. Days after starring in Clermont's Top 14 final win over Toulon in 2017, he scored a try on his debut for the France national team against South Africa.

In 2019, Damian moved from outside centre to the wing as part of an exciting young France team featuring Antoine Dupont, Romain Ntamack and Grégory Alldritt. That year, Les Bleus (The Blues) were knocked out in the Men's Rugby World Cup quarter-finals, but they were building towards a brighter future.

With more space to show off his skills, Damian scored three tries as France won a 2022 Six Nations Grand Slam, and then scored fourteen in just eleven international matches in 2023. His breakout year began with five tries in the Six Nations and ended with six in the Men's Rugby World Cup, including the opening try of the tournament as France beat New Zealand.

Damian is fast but not Habana-fast, and he's strong but not Lomu-strong – so what makes him such a special winger? Two things, really:

1. Firstly, he has a magical ability to get away from defenders. One of the reasons why Damian is so hard to stop is because you never quite know what he's going to do next. Across all France matches in 2023, he somehow managed to escape from 75 per cent of tackles!
2. His other super power is to always be in the right place at the right time. Since his

international debut in 2017, he has scored more than any other player in the world. While helping France to win the Six Nations in 2025, Damian also became France's joint all-time leading try-scorer (with the legendary Serge Blanco), and he's still in his 20s!

It's unlikely that Damian will ever be a top defender; that's just not his style, and he's such a dangerous attacker that he can get away with a few missed tackles. "Damian is a free spirit," says his former youth coach Thomas Lièvremont. "I can't think of anyone to whom I can compare him. He's a unique player."

MAGGIE'S INSIGHTS

Damian is the definition of "French flair"! He just loves to attack and if you give him space, he will take it in a flash. He is so exciting to watch and he makes scoring tries a work of art, which is why the France fans love him so much!

MODERN HERO

DUHAN VAN DER MERWE
BACK THREE

- POSITION **WINGER**
- DATE OF BIRTH **4 JUNE 1995**
- COUNTRY **SCOTLAND**
- CLUBS **BLUE BULLS, MONTPELLIER, EDINBURGH, WORCESTER WARRIORS**
- SUPERSTAR MOMENT **SCORING A HAT-TRICK OF TRIES AGAINST ENGLAND IN THE 2024 SIX NATIONS**
- FUN FACT **DUHAN'S OLDER BROTHER, AKKER, WON THREE CAPS FOR SOUTH AFRICA IN 2018 AS A HOOKER.**

DUHAN VAN DER MERWE

Duhan van der Merwe decided to take the long route to the top of world rugby, but fortunately for him he's one of the fastest players around!

Growing up in South Africa, Duhan's dream was to play for his country, and as a teenager, he was right on track. "But when I hit twenty things weren't working out the way I wanted them to," he says. "I had a lot of injuries that set me back and I found myself stuck in a bit of a rut."

So, Duhan took the brave decision to move to Europe: first to French club Montpellier, and then to Scottish club Edinburgh in 2017, where he finally found his best form again. He scored ten tries in his first season, then ten more in his second, and by the end of his third, he had been called up to play for Scotland!

You see in international rugby, the rule was that after living in a country for three years, you can play for their national team, so despite his love for South Africa, Duhan said yes, and began wearing the Scotland shirt with pride.

Duhan scored a try on his Scotland debut against Georgia, and then five more during the

2021 Six Nations, including the winners against France and England, which made him an instant Scottish hero! A few months later, he also played in all three Tests for the British and Irish Lions, as they were defeated by his beloved South Africa.

After that unforgettable first year of international rugby, Duhan didn't just relax and enjoy himself; no, he carried on working hard to improve his game, even hiring a mental skills coach to help him with his confidence and concentration.

While he's probably best known for his electric pace, at 1.93 metres (6 ft 4 in) and 106 kg, Duhan also has the power to burst through any defender in the game, and he's more than happy to use it. "I like the physical side of things," he says. "Sometimes I just have to offer up my body and run into big forwards and if I have to do that for the team then I will do it any time of the day."

Duhan's favourite opponents? Definitely England. In 2023, he scored twice against them, including one of the best Six Nations tries of all time, where he ran from his own half to the try line, past five attempted tackles. Then a year later in the 2024 Six Nations, Duhan went one better and scored a hat-trick! "I guess I just wake up and start feeling like scoring tries against England," he joked afterwards. He grabbed yet another try when the two teams met in 2025, but this time, it wasn't enough to save Scotland from defeat.

True, but Duhan does try-scoring so brilliantly – better than any other Scotland player ever, in fact. Yes, in 2024, he became his adopted country's all-time leading try-scorer. South Africa's loss was certainly Scotland's gain.

MAGGIE'S INSIGHTS

Duhan really has it all: the size and strength of a forward, plus the speed and skill of a back. He's a real finisher, who beats defenders for fun. I love watching him play, although not against England, because he always has his best game and scores lots of tries!

★ ENTERTAINER ★

ILONA MAHER
BACK THREE

POSITION **WINGER, OUTSIDE CENTRE**

DATE OF BIRTH **12 AUGUST 1996**

COUNTRY **USA**

CLUBS **BRISTOL BEARS**

SUPERSTAR MOMENT **WINNING A BRONZE MEDAL IN WOMEN'S RUGBY SEVENS AT THE 2024 PARIS OLYMPICS**

FUN FACT **ON US TV SHOW *DANCING WITH THE STARS*, ILONA BECAME THE FIRST FEMALE TO EVER LIFT HER MALE PARTNER IN THE AIR!**

ILONA MAHER

Defence-busting runs, booming tackles, dancing feet and hilarious TikTok videos – USA star Ilona Maher really is the ultimate entertainer.

Growing up in Vermont, USA, Ilona tried different sports at school: hockey, basketball, softball. While she enjoyed them all, none of them felt quite right, and so her dad had an idea: what about rugby? He had played the game himself and he thought Ilona might love it too, and guess what! She did!

Ilona only started her rugby journey at the age of seventeen, but five years later, she was making her international debut for the USA women's rugby sevens team, and then two years after that, she was setting off for Tokyo to compete at the 2020 Summer Olympics!

There, Ilona became a sporting superstar, and not just for the three speedy tries she scored for Team USA. With no spectators allowed at the Games due to Covid-19, Ilona entertained rugby fans all over the world with funny behind-the-scenes videos that quickly went viral.

From there, her fame continued to grow: both

on social media and in the world of rugby. With her size and strength, Ilona usually played in the front row as a hooker in rugby sevens, but she also had the explosive pace and power to break away and attack. At the 2022 Women's Rugby World Cup Sevens, she helped the USA Eagles to reach the semi-finals, and then at the 2024 Summer Olympics in Paris, she scored three more tries as the Eagles shocked Great Britain and Australia to win the Bronze Medal!

And while she was starring on the pitch for her country, Ilona also continued to post online. Some of her videos were silly, but others were more serious, dealing with important issues, such as mental health, gender equality and body positivity. Ilona wanted to show the world that she was proud to be so strong and powerful, and to inspire others to feel the same way. "All body types are beautiful and can do amazing things," she said. "So truly see yourself in these athletes and know that you can do it too."

By the end of her second Olympics, Ilona was the world's most popular rugby player on Instagram, with way more followers than even World Rugby itself! So what would she do next? Well, after finishing second on the reality TV show *Dancing with the Stars*, she took on her next challenge: switching to fifteens in time to represent the USA at the next Women's Rugby World Cup!

To prepare, Ilona signed a three-month contract with English club Bristol Bears in January 2025. Playing on the wing, she scored four tries in just seven games, but as the Bears captain Amber Reed says, "The impact that she's had on the game as a whole is pretty phenomenal."

Yes, "Maher Mania" led to record crowds and increased interest in the Premiership Women's Rugby (PWR) league because whatever she's doing, Ilona is always worth watching.

MAGGIE'S INSIGHTS

I met Ilona when I was filming a TV programme. She exuded confidence. Every word carried weight, and she backed it up with her presence. We spoke about social media, women's sport, the Women's Rugby World Cup and our hopes for the future. After our interview I left feeling inspired, not just by what she is doing to raise the profile of the sport but her resilience and determination to show rugby fans that she is much more than just a social media sensation.

★ GAMECHANGER ★

JASON ROBINSON

BACK THREE

POSITION **FULL-BACK, WINGER**

DATE OF BIRTH **30 JULY 1974**

COUNTRY **ENGLAND**

CLUBS **BATH, SALE SHARKS**

SUPERSTAR MOMENT **SCORING A TRY AS ENGLAND WON THE 2003 MEN'S RUGBY WORLD CUP FINAL**

FUN FACT **HIS NICKNAME WAS "BILLY WHIZZ", AFTER A CHARACTER IN THE *BEANO* COMICS WHO COULD RUN REALLY FAST!**

JASON ROBINSON

On the wing or at full-back, in rugby union or league, Jason Robinson had the electric speed and step to change any game.

Jason grew up in Leeds, at the heart of English rugby league. "I never knew anything about rugby union," he admits. "It wasn't mentioned around these streets." Jason's dream was to play for his local professional club, Leeds Rhinos, but when they turned him down, he signed for the Wigan Warriors instead in 1991.

There, Jason became one of rugby league's most famous and successful superstars, until in 2000, he made the big, bold decision to switch to rugby union. He signed for Sale Sharks, knowing that Clive Woodward, the coach of the England national team, wanted him to be a part of his back three at the 2003 Men's Rugby World Cup. *Ooooh*, exciting!

"I'd been in the game [league] for a long time, won everything, but I think sometimes you've got to test yourself," Jason said, "and by playing rugby union at that level, it certainly was a challenge."

In 2001, he became only the second player

ever to go from Team GB in rugby league to the England rugby union team. So, would he be as successful in his second sport? Jason's new teammates were blown away by his professional attitude and his many attacking talents. They loved his balance, his acceleration, his sidestep and "his ability to beat players both ways, and make 90-degree direction changes without losing speed", as Jonny Wilkinson described it.

In the first Test of the 2001 British and Irish Lions tour of Australia, Jason got the ball on the left wing and danced his way to the try line after just three minutes. He scored again in the third Test too. Wow, he was making the switch to rugby union look so easy!

In the 2003 Men's Rugby World Cup group stage, Jason scored three tries as a winger, but for England's quarter-final against Wales, he was picked to play at full-back instead. Really? At just 1.73 metres (5 ft 8 in), how was he going to battle for the high-ball? By using his amazing three-metre jump to outleap much taller opponents! And when he got the ball at the back, Jason then had more space ahead to race into. *ZOOM!* – he weaved his way past six players and set up Will Greenwood to score.

For the semi-final and final, Jason was back on the wing, and in the biggest game against Australia, he sped away to score his biggest try. When the final whistle blew, England were the winners, and Jason was a World Champion!

And the magical moments didn't end there. In 2004, Jason became his country's first-ever Black captain, and after retiring in 2005, he then returned to star at full-back at the 2007 Men's Rugby World Cup. Although England lost in the final this time, Jason walked away from the game as a true rugby legend.

MAGGIE'S INSIGHTS

Everything Jason touched turned to gold. He would glide across the pitch, past defenders, like a skater on ice. He inspired so many to follow in his footsteps and showed that it is possible to switch from one sport to another if you truly believe in yourself.

GAMECHANGER

SHANE WILLIAMS
BACK THREE

POSITION **WINGER**

DATE OF BIRTH **26 FEBRUARY 1977**

COUNTRY **WALES**

CLUBS **NEATH, OSPREYS, MITSUBISHI**

SUPERSTAR MOMENT **WINNING A SIX NATIONS GRAND SLAM AND WORLD RUGBY MEN'S PLAYER OF THE YEAR AWARD IN 2008**

FUN FACT **SHANE'S DREAM JOB AS A KID? STUNTMAN. HE'S CERTAINLY GOT THE COURAGE AND AGILITY FOR IT!**

SHANE WILLIAMS

They say rugby is a sport for all shapes and sizes, but there were several times when Shane Williams was told that he was too small to become a top player. So, did he listen to the doubters? No, he kept going until he changed the game for ever.

Growing up in South Wales, Shane always loved rugby, but due to his size, he was encouraged to focus on football and gymnastics instead. It was only later, as a teenager, that Shane began shining as a rugby scrum-half, and he signed his first professional contract with Neath in 1998.

The club already had a scrum-half, though, so what other positions could Shane play? Hmmm, with his brilliant balance from years of gymnastics, plus his explosive speed and try-scoring skills, what about ... WINGER?

ZOOM! In his new role, Shane was ready to fly for Wales. At the 2000 Six Nations, he scored a try against Italy, and then two more against Scotland. Surely he was all set to become his country's star winger now? But no, the Wales coach wanted bigger, more powerful players in the back three.

Shane? Nope, too small, and when he tried to build extra muscle, he kept getting injured.

"I was fed up and felt like quitting," he admits. But instead he kept working hard and eventually made the Wales squad for the 2003 Men's Rugby World Cup. Originally, he was selected as the third-choice scrum-half, but for the final group game versus New Zealand, Shane got another chance to star on the wing.

Impressing against the All Blacks is never an easy task, but Shane succeeded. First, his breakaway run helped set up a try, and then he darted through a gap in the defence and dived over the try line himself. Maybe being small wasn't such a bad thing, after all!

This time, Shane really was all set to become his country's star winger. In 2005, he scored Wales' winning try against England as they won a Six Nations Grand Slam, and in 2008, they did it again, plus Shane became his country's all-time leading try-scorer AND the World Rugby Men's Player of the Year!

At the 2011 Men's Rugby World Cup, Shane scored three more tries to set a new tournament record for Wales, and most importantly, to help them reach the semi-finals for the first time since 1987. Then two months later, in the last of his 87 international appearances, Shane scored the last of his 58 international tries with the final move of the match against Australia. What a perfect way to say goodbye!

"I really still can't get over the fact that I've won Grand Slams, and I've achieved so much," he said as he retired. "I was fed up of people telling me I was too small... I wanted people to say, "Oh that Shane Williams – he was a good player."

Well, congratulations, "Welsh Wizard" – mission accomplished, although we'll upgrade "good" to "great", if that's OK with you!

MAGGIE'S INSIGHTS

Shane was never scared to take players on, even when they were twice his size. I remember him making his debut for Wales when he was 22 and he was a lightweight compared to the player he was up against, but his speed and footwork were outstanding. In the modern game, wingers are getting bigger, but Shane showed you don't have to be massive to be mighty.

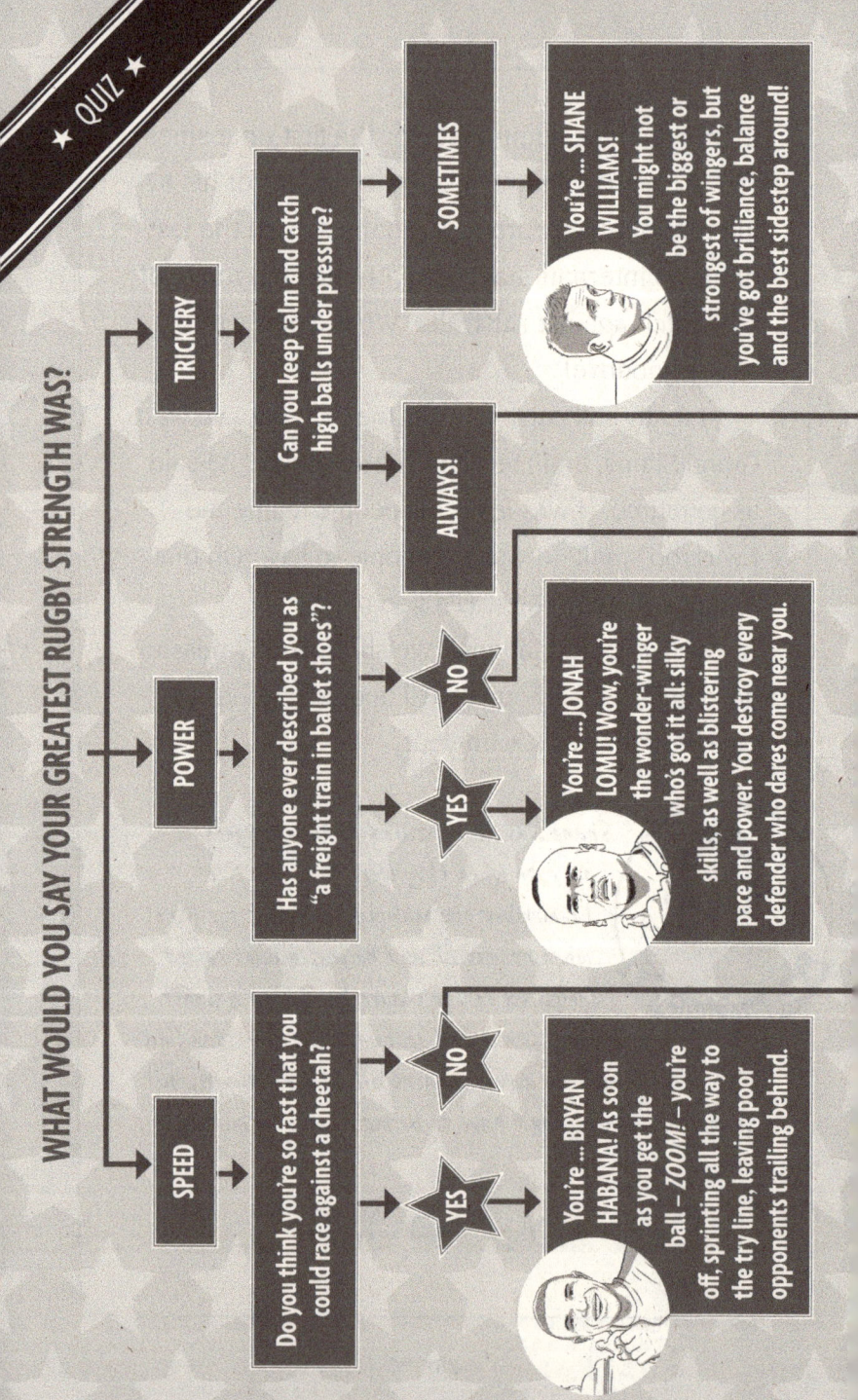

If you had to play a different kind of rugby, which would you go for?

→ **RUGBY SEVENS**

You're ... ELLIE KILDUNNE! From full-back, you just get the ball and *goooo*, dancing your way through the defence with your excellent speed and step.

→ **RUGBY LEAGUE**

You're ... JASON ROBINSON! Whether you're playing on the wing or at full-back, you've got the balance, acceleration, and sidestep to be a back three superstar.

Are you all about attack, or do you like to defend, too?

→ **LIKE TO DEFEND, TOO**

You're ... ILONA MAHER! Yes, you love scoring tries, but you also love stopping them too, using your explosive pace and power to make crucial, crunching tackles.

→ **ALL ABOUT ATTACK**

After speed, what would you say your next greatest strength is?

→ **POWER!**

You're ... DUHAN VAN DER MERWE! While you're best known for your electric pace, you also have the size and strength to burst past any defender in the game.

→ **TRICKERY**

You're ... PORTIA WOODMAN! Sprinting is what you do best, but if there are opponents in your way, you're brilliant at weaving your way through tackles, too.

You're ... DAMIAN PENAUD! Defending's not really your style; you're a dangerous attacker with a magical ability to get away from defenders, and an amazing eye for the try line.

GAME OVER!

That's it, the final whistle has blown, and it's all over for *Ultimate Rugby Superstars*!

We hope you've enjoyed reading the inspiring stories of 50 of the game's most entertaining and successful players. Rugby really is an amazing sport, isn't it? The powerful scrums, the weaving runs; the offload flicks and the clever kicks; but above all, the exciting drama that comes when two teams battle it out to try and score more points than each other. What's not to love about that?!

Hopefully we've also proved that rugby really isn't that complicated, especially now that you know your rucks from your mauls, and your drop kicks from your box kicks.

But before we say goodbye and good luck on your own rugby journey, it's time for you to answer the ultimate question – after learning about lots of different styles, positions and personalities: which kind of rugby superstar would you like to be?

 **Ox Nché**, winning lots of scrums with your powerful pushing?

Zoe Aldcroft, leading the way in the lineout and beyond?

 **Pieter-Steph du Toit**, making tackles and forcing turnovers all over the field?

Antoine Dupont, running the show with your perfect passing?

 **Dan Carter**, controlling the game and kicking your team to glory?

Emily Scarratt, blowing teams away with your speed and skill, in attack and defence?

 **Jonah Lomu**, flying through tackle after tackle and all the way to the try line?

Whatever you decide, we really hope that this book will inspire you to grab a rugby ball and have a great time playing the game with your friends. So, who wants to kick off?

ACKNOWLEDGEMENTS

First of all, a big thanks to Maggie for being such a superstar teammate. They say don't meet your heroes, but it's been an honour and a pleasure to work with you. Next up, thanks go to our editors, Daisy Jellicoe and Rachel Cooke, and our agent, Nick Walters, for guiding us all the way from a plan to an actual book.

My heartiest rugby cheers also go to: illustrator extraordinaire Dan Leydon; the King Edward VI rugby team 2005–06; Mum, for making it very clear that she never wanted me to play rugby; Dad, for passing on his love of the Wales team; Martin, Toby and Basty, for getting me back into the sport; and finally, Iona, Arlo and Lila, for all their love and support.

M.O.

I, too, would like to thank my teammate and partner in crime, Matt, for making this possible. Your enthusiasm and way with words is infectious. I've enjoyed the journey and I owe that to you. My agent, Julia Hutton – what can I say?! You've been by my side since the launch of my professional career. I could not have done this without you. It was your idea to make this happen and I'm so pleased we've finally done it!

Thank you to my wife, Marcella, and beautiful kids, Artie and Willow, for giving me the confidence I need each day, to never stop making a difference and approaching each day with a smile.

Finally, thank you to you, for picking up and reading this book. I hope you enjoy it, learn from it, and feel inspired by the stories you have read.

M.A.

ABOUT THE AUTHORS

Matt Oldfield has never been a rugby superstar himself, but he loves watching other people play the game, and now writing about it too. Matt is also the co-author of the bestselling Ultimate Football Heroes and Football GOAT series, as well as the author of *Johnny Ball: Accidental Football Genius* and *Unbelievable Football*, which won the *Telegraph* Children's Sports Book of the Year in 2020. This is his second book about his other favourite sports, following *Ultimate Cricket Superstars*.

Maggie Alphonsi is a rugby superstar, who transformed women's rugby. She won the 2014 Women's Rugby World Cup with England in 2014 and has won seven consecutive Six Nations titles. She was also named Women's Rugby Player of the Year in 2006 and inducted into the World Rugby Hall of Fame. Now retired, she remains a senior leader in the sport and continues to inspire in her other role as a broadcaster and TV pundit, regularly commentating on men's and women's rugby. Maggie is also the co-author of *Winning the Fight*, her autobiography.